THE TASTES OF CALIFORNIA WINE COUNTRY

NORTH COAST

A Restaurant Guide & Restaurant Recipe Cookbook

A Bed & Breakfast Guide
& Bed & Breakfast Recipe Cookbook
Wine & Winery Guide

Written & Compiled by Sonnie Imes

Printed in the United States of America
Library of Congress Registration Number
TX2-116-607

International Standard Book Number
0-934181-04-7

This book is dedicated to
all Black Diamonds.

NAPA VALLEY

Chardonnay

PRODUCED & BOTTLED BY RAYMOND VINEYARD & CELLAR
ST. HELENA, CALIFORNIA / TABLE WINE

Rich apple and pear aromas are spiced with French oak.
The mouth-filling, well-balanced fruit and oak flavors
follow through to a long, crisp satisfying finish.

An excellent complement to soft-ripening cheeses, lobster bisque,
California-grilled poultry and fish, seafood pastas and
salmon with a butter-based sauce. Also delightful on its own.

Table of Contents

6

9

Caper Sauce
Zucchini and Ham Frittata
Parisian Potatoes
Hungarian Apple Strudel
Hungarian Apple Strudel Filling

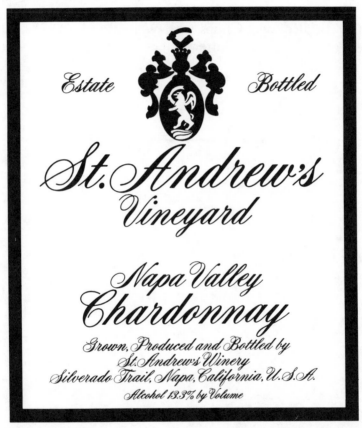

Estate   *Bottled*

St. Andrew's Vineyard

Napa Valley Chardonnay

Grown, Produced and Bottled by
St. Andrew's Winery
Silverado Trail, Napa, California, U.S.A.
Alcohol 13.3% by Volume

Rich apple and blossom aromas predominate with hints of fig
and pineapple and spicy oak in a complex nose.
The Estate Chardonnays of St. Andrew's Vineyards are
well-structured, with a long finish and lingering flavors
which soften elegantly with aging.

The rich apple and barrel spice suggest use with most seafood
and pasta dishes, or cheese and white-sauce offerings.
The richness and structure on the palate are a delight with
lamb and lighter meat dishes.

13

SAN FRANCISCO

1 SQUARE ONE
2 INN AT THE OPERA
3 ERNIE'S
4 HAYES ST. GRILL
5 THE INN SAN FRANCISCO
6 VICTORIAN INN ON THE PARK
7 MASA'S
8 THE MONTE CRISTO

S Q U A R E   O N E

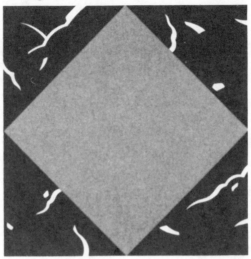

190 Pacific Avenue • San Francisco, California 94111
(415) 788-1110
Hours: 11:30 a.m.-2:30 p.m., Lunch, Mon.-Fri.
5:30 p.m.-10:00 p.m., Dinner, Mon.-Thurs.
5:30 p.m.-10:30 p.m., Dinner, Fri. and Sat.
5:00 p.m.-9:30 p.m., Dinner, Sunday
Prices: Moderate
Reservations: Suggested
Specialties: International and Mediterranean

The exciting Square One Restaurant, located in the heart of San Francisco's financial district is the perfect showcase for Chef Joyce Goldstein's innovative cooking talents. Each day she makes up a new menu using the freshest in available vegetables, meats and seafood, to create a wide array of International classics and Mediterranean specialties that will keep the most jaded person's palate piqued. The extensive wine list offers excellent California wines and some rare imported vintages, ten of which can be sampled by the glass or half glass. Elegant entrees and fine wines carefully presented by a thoughtful and efficient staff provide one of the most enjoyable dining experiences in the city.

17

Broccoli Soup with White Beans, Pasta and Parmesan

½ c. small white beans, soaked overnight in 2 c. water
olive oil
½ c. small pasta shells
6 T. butter
2 medium onions, diced
2 heads of broccoli, tough stems discarded, the rest cut up
   into 2" chunks
4 c. chicken stock (or a bit more)
salt, pepper to taste
grated Parmesan cheese

Drain the white beans and rinse well. Cover with 2 c. fresh cold water and bring to a boil. Lower the heat and simmer about 30 minutes, until beans are tender but not mushy. Drain, and toss with a good quality virgin olive oil. Cook the pasta shells in 4 c. boiling salted water, until al dente. Drain the pasta and toss with oil.

Melt the butter in a 3 qt. saucepan. Add the onions and saute until the onions are transparent. Add the chopped broccoli and cover with chicken stock. Bring to a boil. Simmer until broccoli is very tender. Puree soup in blender or processor. Add salt and pepper. Just before serving add the white beans and pasta shells. Serve garnished with grated Parmesan cheese. You may want to add more chicken stock if the soup seems too thick. If broccoli is too cabbagy in flavor, add a T. of lemon juice for balance.

Serves 8-10

Square One Restaurant's Tomato Soup

¼ lb. butter
2 large yellow onions, sliced
12 large beefsteak tomatoes
salt and pepper to taste

Slice butter into saucepan and sweat onions. Cut beefsteak or other flavorful tomatoes into quarters. Add tomatoes to the soften-ed onions. Stir occasionally, to prevent scorching. Cook until tomatoes are completely broken down and have given off a great deal of liquid.
Puree the onions and tomatoes in the blender. Pass through a food mill to remove seeds and excessive peel. Season to taste with salt and pepper.
Serve garnished with one of the following:

creme fraiche* and chopped basil or mint
orange peel flavored cream
croutons and Parmesan
crouton with goat cheese

You may add a walnut sized piece of ginger root, grated, to the onions while sauteeing for another variation.

Serves 4-6

*See Glossary
19

Chicken "Fricassee" with Mushrooms, Peas, Onions and Cream

4 large, whole chicken breasts, skinned and boned, cut into
   strips 1" x 2"
olive oil
¼ lb. butter
2 yellow onions, diced
½ lb. mushrooms, sliced about ¼" thick
2 c. cream
3 egg yolks
nutmeg
1 c. peas, blanched
salt and pepper
1 lb. fresh egg fettuccine
grated Parmesan cheese

Heat large saute pan. Brown the chicken quickly, over high heat
in olive oil, but do not cook through (about 80% done). Remove
the chicken from the pan. Melt the butter in the pan. Cook the
onions for 2-4 minutes, until transparent. Add mushrooms and
cook 2 minutes more.

Return chicken to pan. Add the cream which has been combined with egg yolks and a pinch of nutmeg. Cook over low heat
for two minutes. Add peas and heat through. Adjust seasoning.
Serve with cooked fettuccine. Sprinkle with Parmesan cheese.

Serves 4-6

Rigatoni with Fennel Sausage, Onions, Greens and Red Peppers

1 lb. rigatoni (De Cecco or other imported Italian dry pasta)
olive oil, light
1 lb. fennel sausage, casings removed
2 medium red onions, sliced ¼" thick
3 small red bell peppers, seeded and sliced ¼" thick
4 c. swiss chard, well washed, cut into ½" wide strips
splash of chicken stock or red wine vinegar, 2 T.
4-6 cloves garlic, minced fine

Bring a large pot of 4-6 quarts salted water to a boil. Cook rigatoni
until al dente (about 7-10 minutes), depending on the brand.
Meanwhile, in a large deep saute pan, heat enough olive oil to
film the bottom of the pan. Saute the crumbled sausage until it
is lightly browned. Set aside.
Saute the onions and peppers until tender but not soft. Add swiss
chard, a splash of stock or red wine vinegar, and stir until greens
are somewhat wilted. Return sausage to the pan, add the garlic
and heat for a few minutes. Adjust seasoning to taste. Drain the
rigatoni and mix well with the sauce.
Ideally the sauce and the pasta will be ready at the same time.
If you worry about timing, cook the sauce part way, hold, cook
the pasta, and then heat the sauce for one minute while pasta
is draining.

Serves 4

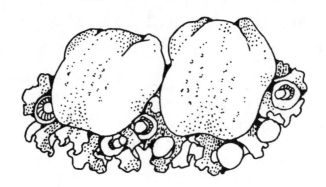

Pollo al Rosmarino
(Grilled Little Chicken with Rosemary)

6 broiler or baby chickens (poussin) about 1 lb. each
8 T. coarsely chopped fresh rosemary
12 cloves garlic, finely minced
3 T. coarsely ground black pepper
½ c. lemon juice
2 c. olive oil, or enough to cover the chickens
lemon wedges

Combine all ingredients except chicken. Marinate the chickens in the above mixture for 24 hours, in a shallow non-corrosive dish. Keep refrigerated and turn occasionally. Bring to room temperature just before cooking.
Preheat broiler to high (or fire up the outdoor charcoal grill). Sprinkle the birds with salt and pepper. Grill, skin side up (away from the heat) for 5 minutes. Then turn and cook until done—about another 3-5 minutes, depending upon the heat of your grill or broiler. Serve with a lemon wedge.

Serves 6

Salmone alla Giapponese
(Salmon, Japanese Style)

½ c. soy sauce
1 c. white vermouth or sake
2 c. chicken stock
2 t. minced garlic
2 T. fresh grated ginger root (or more)
¼ lb. sweet butter
salmon fillets (6-8 oz. per serving)
lemon wedges

Bring the first 5 ingredients to a boil. Reduce heat to a simmer and cook about 30 minutes. Swirl in ¼ lb. sweet butter. Bake salmon fillets covered with a ladlefull of sauce. Cook until done.* In a saute pan reduce a bit of the sauce along with the pan juices from the salmon. Swirl in a bit more butter. Serve salmon with lemon wedge.

*Cooking time on salmon will vary according to the thickness of the fillets and the heat of your oven. Cook it at 450 degrees for 7 minutes, with the fish fillet cut on a bias.
The sauce can be made ahead of time and will keep for a week or more in the refrigerator.
Use about 6-8 oz. fillet per serving.

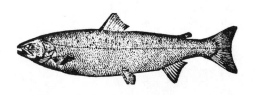

333 Fulton Street • San Francisco, California 94102
(415) 863-8400

Step into exceptional luxury at the Inn At The Opera. Originally designed to cater to the refined tastes of opera stars and their patrons, the grand hotel has been completely remodeled at a cost of $7 million and two years time. In May of 1985 the Inn re-opened its doors and invited San Francisco and the world to experience true elegance and sophistication. Each of the distinctive rooms, from the singles to the deluxe two-bedroom suites, has custom furnishings, room service, evening turndown, complimentary bath toiletries and plush terry robes. The Inn At The Opera also boasts one of the city's best restaurants. The Act IV Lounge, with its overstuffed chairs and sofas, theme paintings, padded tapestry walls, dark, gleaming woods and fireplace of imported green marble, sets a mood usually found only in private clubs. The new Chef, Richard Gac, has carefully planned a menu to satisfy the before and after theater appetite, while titillating the diners who come simply to enjoy the grand cuisine and unparalleled ambiance.

25

Iced Polish Plum Soup

4 lbs. pitted plums, marinated in one fifth port wine,
2 c. orange juice and grated orange peel
2 c. plain yogurt
2 c. sour cream
nutmeg, allspice and cloves

Marinate plums for 24 hours with port wine, orange juice and orange peel. Reserve finely minced rind of one orange. Puree plums in food processor or blender, strain liquid and then with a whisk mix in yogurt, sour cream and orange rind. Add a dash of nutmeg, allspice and cloves to taste. Garnish creatively with a fine tipped squeeze bottle, to make a design on top of the soup.

Serves 6-8

Act IV Duck Liver
Hazelnut Mousse

2 lbs. duck livers
1 pear, diced
1 banana, diced
½ diced red onion
2 T. butter
nutmeg
salt and pepper
dash of Calvados (apple brandy)
¼ lb. butter
½ c. cream
¼ c. hazelnuts
½ c. port wine
2 c. orange juice
1 packet gelatin

Makes 6 3 oz. ramekin molds

Saute livers, pear, banana and red onion in butter until done. Add nutmeg, salt and pepper to taste. Flambe in Calvados. for one hour. Whip cream, then fold in hazelnuts and add to chilled liver mixture.

Place port wine and orange juice in sauce pan and heat until boiling. Add one envelope gelatin that has been dissolved in water. Chill. When syrupy, spoon on top of liver mixture in ramekins. Chill until set.

Serves 6

Salad Giverny

assorted baby lettuces (6 heads)
fresh herbs (dill, lemon thyme, mint
  and purple basil)
nasturtium blossoms, organic rose petals, fresh
  crenshaw melon, yellow pear tomatoes,
  toasted crushed hazelnuts, domestic beluga caviar

Arrange the different lettuces, torn gently by hand, herbs,
blossoms, rose petals, melon cut in triangles, tomatoes and
hazelnuts into a creative expression on 4-6 chilled plates. Sprinkle
with Hazelnut Vinaigrette (recipe follows) and place caviar on
petals and melon triangles.

Serves 4-6

Hazelnut Vinaigrette

Combine with whisk 2 c. hazelnut oil, 1 c. rice vinegar, juice of
1 orange, cracked pepper to taste and finely chopped fresh herbs.
Chill.

28

Petrale Sole Macademia
with Salmon Caviar

4 6 oz. portions of East Coast Fillet of Sole
½ c. flour
4 eggs, beaten
one cup pulverized baked macademia nuts
8 oz. melted butter
2½ lbs. salmon caviar
½ dozen chives

Buerre Rouge:

2 c. red wine
½ c. rice vinegar
1 bay leaf
1 T. black peppercorns
1 T. minced red onion
½ c. heavy cream
¾ c. butter at room temperature

To prepare Buerre Rouge:
In a saucepan reduce red wine, rice vinegar, bay leaf, black peppercorn, red onion to ⅔ of volume, extract liquid through strainer
into another saucepan. Add heavy cream with a whisk and reduce
to half. Slice butter into cubes and add in pieces one by one with
a whisk until emulsified. Set aside.
Dredge sole in flour, then dip in eggs, then in macademia nuts.
Heat a saute pan to a very hot degree, and add butter. Brown
sole on both sides and set aside. Spoon Buerre Rouge on bottom
of heated plate. Place sole on top, and top that with a large T.
of salmon caviar. Garnish with two long chives placed on top
of caviar horizontally. Any vegetable preparation you serve with
this should be blanched in salted boiling water only!
This recipe is fondly dedicated to Mr. James E. Brennan and
Robert F. Begley.

       Serves 4-6

Black Mission Figs with Orange Cream Cheese

3 ripe figs per guest
½ lb. cream cheese
dash Grand Marnier
zest of 1 lime
juice from 1 orange, strained
1 T. brown sugar

Chill dessert plates. Cut the tops off figs and slice ¾ of the way down vertically once, and then horizontally once. Gently push open and arrange on plate.
Whip in blender or food processor cream cheese, Grand Marnier, lime zest, juice of 1 orange, and brown sugar. Blend and serve either on top of figs or separately.

Serves 4-6

847 Montgomery Street • San Francisco, California 94133
(415) 397-5969
Hours: 5:30 p.m.-10:30 p.m. Dinner, seven days a week
Closed all major holidays
Credit Cards: All Major
Prices: Expensive
Reservations: Required
Specialties: Contemporary French

Lauded by critics and touted by celebrities, the award winning Ernie's Restaurant in San Francisco serves unsurpassed contemporary French cuisine under the watchful eye of the Gotti brothers (Victor and Roland) and Chef Bruno Tison. Fifty-two years and 2 generations of Gottis have created a restaurant that has become the standard by which others are measured. Silver service on each table, elegant silk brocade walls, a beautiful stained glass back bar and a staff trained to anticipate and fulfill diners' desires makes Ernie's a must for fledgling gourmets and seasoned epicureans alike. Chef Bruno, who has studied and trained with some of the more notable names in the culinary world, has outstripped his teachers and found his own place in the sun. Every dish is a picture perfect creation that does not fail to follow through with consistent quality and tantalizing combinations. The wide selection of excellent domestic vintages on the acclaimed wine list is considered the best of California and has won awards six years running for its excellence and depth. Ernie's truly represents the epitome of fine dining in San Francisco.

31

Dry Braised Fresh Tuna
(Served with a Ragout of Baby Eggplant and Ginger)

¾ lb. fresh tuna, cut into ½" thick strips
salt
white pepper
2 Japanese (baby) eggplants
½ c. flour
2 c. vegetable oil
1 lb. clams
2 c. white wine
2 shallots, chopped
4 oz. cream
3 T. butter
1-2 T. clarified butter
2-3 T. olive oil
1 ginger root, peeled and finely sliced
½ c. port
a few sprigs fresh cilantro

Season the tuna lightly with salt and white pepper; set aside. Cut the eggplants in rounds (crosswise) about ½" thick; salt and flour them lightly. Heat 2 c. vegetable oil in deep-fat fryer until very hot. Fry eggplant until golden brown. Drain on paper towels and set aside. Boil clams with the white wine and shallots until clams are fully open and release their juices. Remove clams. Add cream to the wine and shallots and reduce slightly. Thicken with butter to obtain a creamy sauce. Set aside. Marinate the ginger briefly in the port. Drain, dry, and saute the ginger in the clarified butter until crisp. Drain and reserve. Saute the tuna in the olive oil

Dry Braised Fresh Tuna (con't)

until just cooked through, adding more oil if necessary. Heat the eggplant in the oven and re-heat the clam-cream sauce. To serve, arrange the tuna on top of the eggplant, sprinkle with the crisp ginger and coat with the clam sauce. Arrange a few of the whole clams on each plate and decorate with fresh cilantro. Serve very hot.

Serves 2

Trio of Tortellini with Parmesan

1 lb. tortellini
1 T. olive oil
1 tomato, peeled and cut into cubes
1-2 t. fines-herbs (mixed chervil, tarragon and chives)
4 fresh morels, julienned, or
4 shitake mushrooms, julienned
1-2 T. butter
8-10 oz. creme fraiche*
5 t. fresh grated Parmesan cheese (use more if you like)
salt
pepper

Cook the tortellini in boiling salted water with the olive oil until tender. Cool under cold running water. Set aside. Sprinkle the tomato cubes with the herbs. Set aside. Saute the morels (or shitake) in butter and keep warm. Reheat the tortellini with the creme fraiche; sprinkle with Parmesan and salt and pepper to taste. To serve, garnish each portion of tortellini with the tomatoes, and morels (or shitake). Serve hot.

Serves 4

*See Glossary

3 Vegetables

12 leaves of lettuce
½ onion, diced
¼ c. olive oil
1 red bell pepper, diced
1 zucchini, diced
1 eggplant, diced
1 garlic clove, crushed
1 T. fresh thyme
salt and pepper to taste

Preparation:

Blanch the leaves of lettuce and set aside. Saute the onion in olive oil and add the red bell pepper. After a few minutes, add the zucchini, eggplant, crushed garlic, fresh thyme, salt and pepper. Add a small amount of water and finish cooking the vegetables.
Line the inside of a buttered mold with the blanched lettuce leaves and fill with the vegetable "ragout". Seal the top with lettuce leaves. Reheat in steamer and serve.

Serves 4

California Red Berries
in "Creme Brulee" with Brown Sugar

10 egg yolks
4½ oz. sugar
16 oz. (½ liter) cream
1 vanilla bean
1 basket raspberries, lightly rinsed
12-15 strawberries, cleaned and sliced
4 T. brown sugar
a few sprigs of fresh mint

Beat the egg yolks and sugar together until well blended. Heat
the cream with the vanilla bean until boiling; remove bean and
pour the cream over the egg and sugar mixture. Cook for a few
more minutes, then force the mixture through a sieve; set aside.
Arrange the raspberries in the center of each plate and surround
them with the strawberries. Slowly pour the cream mixture
(custard) on top of the berries. Sprinkle with brown sugar and
place under a hot broiler for a few minutes until the sugar melts
slightly. Garnish with fresh mint and serve.

Serves 4

35

Restaurant

MENU

35
36
37
38

Hayes Street Grill

320 Hayes Street • San Francisco, California 94108
(415) 863-5545
Hours: 11:30 a.m.-3:00 p.m. Lunch, Mon.-Fri.
5:00 p.m.-10:00 p.m. Dinner, Mon.-Thur.
5:00 p.m.-11:00 p.m. Dinner, Fri.
6:00 p.m.-11:00 p.m. Dinner, Sat.
Closed Sundays and major holidays
Credit Cards: Visa, M/C
Prices: Moderate
Reservations: Suggested
Specialties: Fresh Fish

Blackboard specials lead the way at the Hayes Street Grill, and from appetizers through dessert everything is as fresh as possible. A lively atmosphere pervades the bar and grill, accented by a dark forest green and white decor, the focal point of which is the ever-present blackboard, guiding hungry diners to culinary paradise. Some days the list announces as many as eleven different fresh fish choices to be mixed and matched with seven different sauces, five of which are featured daily and two are special creations that vary with the whim of the chef. If the fresh catch doesn't spark a bit of curiosity, try a dry-aged New York steak, or sample some grilled Whiskey, Fennel or Boudin Blanc sausages with pommes frites. Accompany the savory entrees with frosty mugs of imported beer or special domestic wines by the glass. Top off your excellent meal with a large slice of Chocolate Torte with Apricots and Walnuts or a smooth and light Creme Brulee. The only problem with dining at the Hayes Street Grill is deciding when to return.

37

Italian Broccoli and Buttermilk Soup

¼ lb. butter
4 medium onions, halved and sliced thinly
8 c. rich chicken stock
6 c. Italian broccoli (Broccoli Rabe), coarsely chopped
salt
pepper
1-2 c. buttermilk

Melt butter in large soup or stock pot. Add sliced onions to butter and saute, covered, until onions are softened and translucent.
Add chicken stock and bring to a simmer, stirring occasionally.
Add Italian broccoli, and cook over a medium flame until the
broccoli is very tender. Working in batches, put the broccoli-
chicken-stock-onion mixture in a food processor and blend
a smooth puree. Put the puree through a sieve, pressing out all
the liquid (a large-holed colander will work best). Season with
salt and pepper to taste and add buttermilk to taste. Serve well
heated.

Serves 8-10

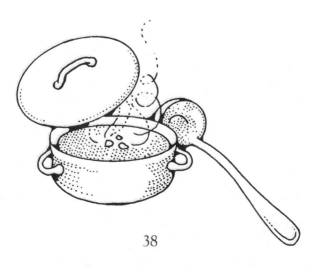

Clams Mariniere

⅔ c. dry white vermouth or dry white wine
1⅓ c. water
⅔ c. shallots, finely chopped
1 bay leaf
4 peppercorns
clams, 1 lb. per person, rinsed well
2 medium cloves of garlic, finely chopped
1½ T. softened butter
4 t. parsley, chopped

Add vermouth or wine, water, shallots, bay leaf and peppercorns together in a saucepan. Simmer gently for half an hour, until shallots are tender. Bring liquid to a boil. Add clams, garlic and softened butter and reduce heat to a simmer. Steam until clams open; add parsley and serve immediately.

Serves 4-6

Mussels with Extra Virgin Olive Oil, Garlic and Lemon

8-10 T. extra virgin olive oil
4 T. lemon juice
2 cloves garlic, finely minced
3 lbs. mussels, cleaned and rinsed
lemon wedges
parsley, finely chopped

In a cold, large saute pan add oil, lemon juice and garlic. Add mussels and cover. Cook over a very low flame until the mussels open and let out their liquid. Serve in individual bowls. Garnish with lemon wedges and chopped parsley.

39

Serves 4-6

Lovely fruit aromas complemented by moderate oak flavors.
Medium bodied with an elegant long finish.

An excellent choice to accompany shellfish, grilled fish,
lightly curried foods and chicken.

Grilled Squid Salad

3 cloves garlic, finely chopped
2 T. lemon juice
salt and pepper
¼ c. olive oil
2 lbs. squid, bodies and tentacles, cleaned well

1 red and 1 yellow pepper, roasted, peeled, seeded,
    and cut into strips
1 T. capers
¼ c. celery, chopped
1 red onion, sliced, roasted in oven with olive oil,
    salt, pepper
Nicoise olives
lemon wedges
handful of arugula

Dressing:
1 c. olive oil
¼ c. lemon juice
¼ c. red wine vinegar
2 t. Worcestershire sauce
1 t. salt
¼ t. pepper
¼ c. basil, chopped
2 T. parsley, chopped
3 medium cloves garlic, finely chopped

Combine garlic, lemon juice, salt and pepper to taste. Add olive
oil slowly; whisk well. Add squid; set aside to marinate. Combine dressing ingredients and set aside. Grill marinated squid over

41

Grilled Squid Salad (con't)

charcoal and cut in rings while still warm. Combine squid with dressing to taste, red and yellow peppers, capers, celery, and roasted red onions. Divide onto serving plates. Garnish with Nicoise olives, lemon wedges and arugula.

Serves 6

Creme Brulee

8 egg yolks
5 T. plus 1 t. sugar
3 c. whipping cream
8 4-oz. porcelain ramekins
brown sugar

Beat egg yolks and sugar only until well mixed (not a ribbon). Bring the whipping cream to a boil. Add scalded cream slowly to egg mixture. Pour mixture into ramekins. Place ramekins in a hot bain marie* at 250 degrees for 1½-2 hours. (Do not pre-heat oven.) Remove from oven, dry on towels, cool and refrigerate. *Before serving:* Cover the cooled custard with a thin layer of brown sugar, and mist with water. With a heated brulee iron (available at cookware stores) caramelize the brown sugar (do not burn it) *or* place the ramekins under a broiler and caramelize sugar. Serve when sugar has cooled and set.

Serves 8

943 South Van Ness Avenue • San Francisco, CA 94110
(415) 641-0188

Step into Victorian splendor at The Inn San Francisco. The impeccably restored Italianate-style Inn was built in 1870 by John English, the "Potato King," who once raised championship horses on the grounds. The grand mansion exudes elegance from its roof-top sun deck with panoramic view, to the beveled glass, ornate woodwork, marble fireplaces and oriental carpets of the grand double parlor where a breakfast buffet and afternoon tea is served each day. The spacious rooms are lavishly decorated with polished brass, marble sinks, antiques and fresh flowers. Union Square, Fisherman's Wharf and a host of other San Francisco sights and delights are easily accessible from the inn and your hosts will gladly recommend and make arrangements to insure each visit is a memorable one.

43

Date Cake

½ lb. dates
1 t. baking soda
1 c. boiling water
1 T. butter
1 c. sugar
1 egg, slightly beaten
½ c. nut meats (walnut is our favorite)
1¼ c. cake flour, sifted

Place dates in saucepan; sprinkle soda over them and pour on boiling water. Let cool. Cream butter; beat in sugar, then add slightly beaten egg and beat well. Add dates, nut meats and flour. Bake in greased loaf pan 30 minutes at 325 degrees.

Serves 12

Swedish Spice Cake

1 egg, slightly beaten
1 c. sugar
¼ c. shortening
1 t. baking soda
1 T. water
1 c. raisins, cooked in 1¼ c. water 20 minutes,
   strain and save water
¾ water from raisins
1 t. allspice
1 t. nutmeg
¼ t. cloves
1 t. cinnamon

44

Swedish Spice Cake (con't)

½ t. salt
1½ c. flour, sift after measuring

Mix in order given. Bake at 375 degrees in a buttered and floured 1½ or 2 quart pan approximately 40 minutes. Cool completely.

Serves 12

German Sour Cream Twists

1 package dry yeast
¼ c. warm water
1 T. vinegar
¾ c. canned milk
1 whole egg
2 egg yolks
3½ c. flour, sifted
1 t. vanilla
½ c. shortening
½ c. butter

Dissolve yeast in warm water, add vinegar to milk. Beat eggs until light and fluffy. Cut shortening and butter into flour. Stir liquid combinations into flour, add vanilla. Chill in refrigerator 2 hours. Divide dough in half and roll on board covered with sugar. Keep rolling and folding in layers. Cut into 1" x 3" strips and twist in a circle. Let rise until double in bulk. Bake at 350 degrees until golden brown.   *Serves 24*

301 Lyon Street • San Francisco, California 94117
(415) 931-1830

The Victorian Inn on the Park, which overlooks Golden Gate Park, is an Inn of exceptional quality and warmth. Innkeepers Lisa and William Benau have captured the essence of 1890's luxury with their charming Bed and Breakfast Inn. Each flower-filled room has a private bath and is uniquely decorated to reflect the best of Victorian San Francisco. An aromatic Continental style breakfast with a complimentary newspaper is served in the oak paneled dining room. Your hosts will be glad to obtain anything from a chauffeured limo, theater tickets or reservations for that special dinner.

47

Cranberry Bread

4 T. unsalted butter
2 c. sugar
2 eggs
4 c. flour
3 t. baking powder
1 t. salt
1 t. baking soda
1 c. orange juice
1½ c. hot water
½ rind of an orange, grated
½ rind of a lemon, grated
2 c. walnuts, chopped
4 c. cranberries

Cream the butter and sugar. Add eggs. In a separate bowl, sift together the dry ingredients. Add dry mixture to butter mixture alternately with the orange juice and water. Add orange and lemon rinds. Add walnuts and cranberries. Place mixture in two greased 3" x 5" x 9" pans and bake at 375 degrees for about 50 minutes.

Serves 30

Bran Muffins

5 c. flour (can use 2½ c. wheat flour)
5 t. soda
2 t. salt
3 c. sugar
4 beaten eggs
1 c. melted shortening
1 quart buttermilk
1 15-oz. box raisin bran
optional: nuts, raisins, drained pineapple,
    chopped dates

Combine all dry ingredients. Mix eggs, shortening and butter-milk. Add raisin bran and mix well. May add any or all of the optional ingredients. Pour in greased muffin pan ⅔ full. Bake at 400 degrees for 15 minutes or until done.

Makes 48 muffins

648 Bush Street • San Francisco, California 94108
(415) 989-7154
Hours: 6:00 p.m. and 9:30 p.m. Dinner, Tues.-Sat.
Two seatings nightly
Credit Cards: Visa, M/C
Prices: Expensive
Reservations: Required three weeks in advance
Specialties: Seafood and Game

For a truly memorable dining experience come to Masa's—a small, stylish, French restaurant in San Francisco; and savor the ultimate in inspired French gourmet cuisine. Exquisitely decorated in subtle shades of burgundy and grey with sparkling crystal and gleaming silver, Masa's is intimate and serene. Chef Bill Galaway, who studied under the venerable Masataka Kobayashi, and Chef Julian Serrano create food that is almost too beautiful to eat. Light sauces, quality ingredients and attention to detail keep "regulars" coming back again and again. To obtain reservations at Masa's please be sure to call exactly three weeks in advance.

51

Souffle Glace Aux Noisettes

¾ c. hazelnuts
6 oz. sugar
3 egg whites
1 c. cream
1½ oz. Amaretto

Make the forms for the individual souffles as follows: fold and cut plain parchment paper into rectangles about 3" tall and 5" wide. Butter one end of the paper and roll it into a cylinder about 1½" in diameter, fixing it with the butter. Set the paper forms upright in ramekins of a slightly larger diameter.

Roast the hazelnuts at 375 degrees F. until the skins char slightly and are loose, and the nuts have a fine aroma. Rub the skins off with a cloth, and dispose of them. Chop the nuts fine. Dissolve the sugar in a little water and cook it until it forms a soft ball. Whip the egg whites, gradually adding the sugar syrup, until smooth, glossy and cool.

Whip the cream until it forms soft peaks, adding the Amaretto just before the cream is finished. Fold in the chopped hazelnuts (reserve some for garnish). Fold the whipped cream mixture into the egg white mixture. Using a pastry bag, pipe the souffle mixture into the prepared paper forms. Freeze. The souffles are ready to serve when they become firm. They remain smooth and creamy. They should not be icy.

Serve on a pool of creme anglaise*, garnished with chopped hazelnuts and a few fresh berries.

Serves 6

*See Glossary

The MONTE CRISTO
Circa 1875

600 Presidio Avenue • San Francisco, California 94115
(415) 931-1875

The brightly painted Monte Cristo caters to all pockets and personalities. The color-ful Bed and Breakfast Inn is convenient to transportation and ten minutes from many points of interest in the busy city of San Francisco. Within a short walking distance you'll find elegantly restored Victorian shops and antique stores. Each of the Inn's rooms is furnished in authentic period pieces and a wonderful breakfast is included.

53

Tomato Sauce

1 c. extra virgin olive oil
8 cloves garlic, chopped
1 lb. plum tomatoes, seeded, peeled, chopped
salt
sugar
pepper
1 bunch sweet basil, shredded

Heat olive oil slightly; saute garlic; add tomatoes. Bring to a simmer; season with salt, sugar and pepper to taste, and let cook 30-40 minutes. Add basil. Cook for another 10 minutes. Serve with pasta. Freezes well.

Mushroom Omelette

Filling:
3 T. butter
1 clove garlic, minced
½ lb. sliced mushrooms
juice of 2 lemons
salt

Heat butter in a skillet; add garlic, mushrooms, lemon juice and salt to taste; saute until limp. Season as desired.
Traditional French omelettes: use 2 eggs. This filling should be enough for 6 2-egg omelettes.

Filling for 6 2-egg omelettes.

MARIN

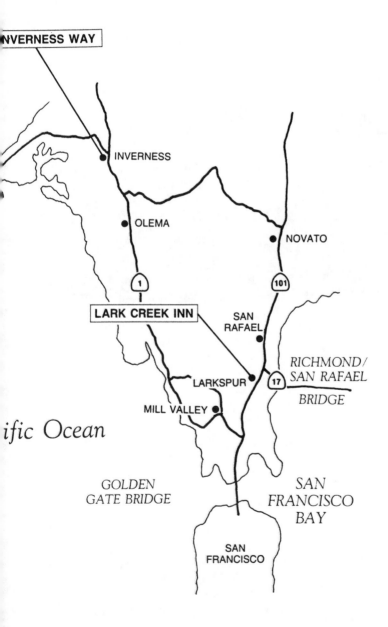

NVERNESS WAY

INVERNESS

OLEMA

NOVATO

1

101

LARK CREEK INN

SAN
RAFAEL

RICHMOND/
SAN RAFAEL

LARKSPUR   17

BRIDGE

MILL VALLEY

ific Ocean

GOLDEN
GATE BRIDGE

SAN
FRANCISCO
BAY

SAN
FRANCISCO

TEN INVERNESS WAY
BED AND BREAKFAST

Ten Inverness Way • Inverness, California 94937
(415) 669-1648

Just about one hour north of San Francisco, in a small hamlet called Inverness, is a special place to stay. Walk up the flower lined flagstone path, past fragrant fruit trees and across the threshold into a warm family home. Five flower scented rooms, each individually decorated, share two large, European style baths. Breakfast in the sun room on hearty fruit topped or banana buckwheat pancakes, French toast, egg specialties or just sip hot coffee and munch on freshly baked breads with homemade jams, while you plan a day of visiting the local points of interest. Tour Johnson's Oyster Farm, see the Miwok Village and Point Reyes National Seashore or stroll along the Earthquake and Woodpecker Nature Trails. During the month of January take a trip to the Lighthouse, and see, far out at sea, the annual migration of the Gray Whales.

57

Whole Wheat Carrot Bread

In large bowl, stir together first 5 ingredients:

1½ c. brown sugar
3 c. whole wheat flour
3 t. cinnamon
1½ t. salt
3½ t. soda
5 carrots
6 eggs
1½ c. oil

Cut 2 carrots into blender. Add the eggs, blend with grated carrots. Pour over dry ingredients. Cut 3 more carrots into blender. Add the oil, blend, and pour over dry ingredients. Stir just until blended. Bake in 3 ungreased loaf pans at 350 degrees for 60 minutes.

Yield: 3 loaves

English Muffin Loaves

Combine:

3 T. yeast
3 c. white flour
3 c. whole wheat flour
4 t. salt
½ t. baking soda
1½ c. dry milk
5 c. very warm tap water
6 c. whole wheat flour
cornmeal

Combine first 6 ingredients. Add the warm tap water, beat well. Add the whole wheat flour. Stir until well combined. Push into 4 bread pans which have been well greased and sprinkled with cornmeal. Let rise in warm place 45 minutes. Bake at 400 degrees for 30 minutes. Remove from pans. Cool.

Yield: 4 loaves

Tomato Frittata

Butter or oil for sauteing
3 c. onion, finely chopped
2 t. basil
1 t. salt
1 lb. can tomatoes, drained and chopped
9 eggs, beaten
2 or 3 c. grated cheese

Saute onions in butter or oil until transparent and very soft. Add basil, salt and tomatoes; simmer, covered, for 5 minutes. Uncover and cook until dry and thick. Set aside to cool. Beat eggs and milk together. Stir in cheese, and then add the tomato mixture. Pour into a greased 9" x 13" pan. Bake at 350 degrees for 45 minutes.

Serves 4-5

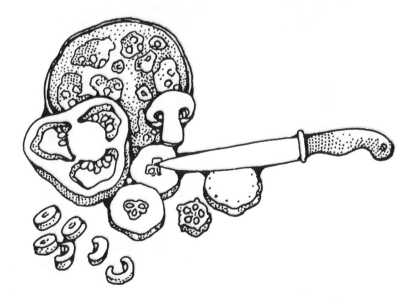

234 Magnolia Avenue • Larkspur, California 94939
(415) 924-7766
Hours: 11:30 a.m.-2:30 p.m. Lunch, Tues.-Sat.
5:30 p.m.-9:30 p.m. Dinner, Tues.-Thurs.
5:30 p.m.-10:30 p.m. Dinner, Fri. and Sat.
5:00 p.m.-9:30 p.m. Dinner, Sunday
11:00 a.m.-2:30 p.m. Sunday Brunch
Credit Cards: All Major
Prices: Moderate
Reservations: Suggested
Specialties: Fresh Seafood, Grilled Meats and Pasta

On the main street of Larkspur behind a cheery yellow and white turn-of-the-century
facade, the Lark Creek Inn serves delighted diners a wide selection of Chef "Sam"
Samanas' finest dishes. Once a lovely old family residence on the banks of the Lark
Creek, the restaurant's colorful history adds to the romantic ambiance of the patiently
restored Victorian mansion. Handcrafted wood panels, modernized antique light
fixtures, matching lampshades, drapes and wallpaper all contribute to an 1880's look.
Savor entrees like Roast Duck with Strawberry or Orange Sauce, fresh grilled Swordfish with fettucini and on the lighter side, Maine Lobster Salad or a creamy avocado
Mousse Samana, under a large glass dome shaded by redwoods during the day and
lit by twinkling stars at night. To accompany Sam's innovative cuisine, a bottle of
choice California wine from a personally selected wine list will round out a meal
fit for a king.

Black Bean Soup

In stock pot combine:
½ bunch celery, chopped
2 carrots, chopped
4 large onions, chopped
2 large leeks, chopped
1 c. sherry wine
2 c. heavy cream
2 lbs. black turtle beans
2 oz. chicken base (paste)
salt
pepper

Let cook for 2 hours, add water if needed. Pour into blender, puree and strain. Put back on heat, until hot. Season with salt and pepper to taste.

Serves 6

Fresh Maine Lobster Salad

Boil lobster. Refrigerate until ready to serve. Clean and cut meat into chunks and arrange on lettuce leaves. Serve with simple vinaigrette dressing, made in ratio of 3 parts oil to 1 part vinegar. Add salt and pepper to taste and chopped fresh herbs to suit your taste.

Grilled Oysters, Cucumber Sauce

12 large oysters
12 strips bacon

Wrap bacon around oysters. Grill until bacon is fully cooked.

Serves 4

Cucumber Sauce

1 large cucumber, seeds removed
½ t. shallots, minced
1 t. salt
1 T. dill weed
½ c. half-and-half
½ t. black pepper

Combine ingredients in blender; blend well.

French Fried Celery Root

1 large celery root

Peel skin off, slice into french fry shape. Cook in hot oil until brown. Use paper towels to dry off excess oil.

Serves 2

Blue Corn Crepes

Crepes:

4 whole eggs
1 c. half-and-half
1 c. Blue cornmeal
oil

Mix eggs, half and half, and corn meal well, beating out any lumps. Pour small quantity of oil into Teflon pan, just to cover. Add 2 oz. of cornmeal mixture (about ¼ c.). With circular motion, spread batter in pan. Cook quickly, turn and cook second side.

Chicken Mixture (to serve 4 people 2 crepes each):

½ large onion, chopped fine
1 T. garlic, minced
2 c. mushrooms, chopped
salt and pepper to taste
2 whole chicken breasts, boned, cooked and chopped fine
1 c. ricotta cheese

Saute onion, garlic and mushrooms until limp. Season with salt and pepper. Remove from heat; add chicken and ricotta cheese.

Basil sauce for crepes:

1 bunch fresh basil, chopped
1 c. water
1 T. chicken base
2 c. heavy cream
1 T. butter
salt and pepper to taste

Cook together in saute pan until reduced by half.

Place chicken mixture evenly on crepes. Fold crepes around, and place on plate, seam side down. Cover with sauce.

Serves 4

Avocado Mousse Samana

6 ripe avocados, peeled and mashed
1½ c. whipping cream
4 T. gelatin
pinch fresh basil
1 t. lemon juice
salt and white pepper
Blend avocado pulp in blender until smooth. Warm a little of the cream and soften gelatin in cream. Add basil, lemon juice, and salt and pepper to taste to pulp in blender. Add cream and gelatin. Blend well. Pour into loaf mold and refrigerate to set.

Dressing:

2 egg yolks
1 T. Dijon mustard
2 T. Barengo Wine Vinegar (or other quality wine vinegar)
salt
pinch of pepper
pinch of flour
1 c. olive oil

Whisk egg yolks with mustard. Add vinegar, salt, pepper, and flour. While whisking, add oil in slow, steady stream.

Garnish:

8-10 spears of endive
8-10 cooked asparagus stalks
baby red lettuce
8-10 slices smoked sturgeon
3-4 cooked large prawns per serving

Preparing Presentation:

Slice mousse into slices approximately ½" thick. Pour a small pool

Avocado Mousse Samana (con't)

of dressing in center of plate. Set mousse slice on dressing. Garnish with spears of endive with thin stalk of asparagus set in groove of leaf; a small cluster of baby red lettuce; thin slices of smoked sturgeon and three or four large prawns. Pass additional dressing.

Makes 8-10 ample servings

Grilled Swordfish on Fettucini

1 swordfish steak
1 T. clarified butter*
½ c. tomatoes, diced
1 T. garlic, minced
splash of white wine
½ c. heavy cream
1 t. fresh basil, chopped
parmesan cheese to taste
salt and pepper to taste
½ to 1 c. cooked fettucini
2-3 asparagus spears, cooked

Grill swordfish steak, according to your favorite method. While fish is grilling, make sauce of the clarified butter, tomatoes, garlic and wine. Cook until reduced by half. Add the cream, basil, parmesan, salt and pepper. Toss with the hot fettucini. Place pasta in center of plate; garnish with cooked asparagus spears. Place swordfish on top of pasta.

Serves 1

*See Glossary

Polenta

6½ c. water
1 T. salt
2 c. coarsely ground cornmeal (polenta)
¼ c. red bell pepper, diced
2 T. fresh basil, chopped
2 T. parsley, chopped

Bring the water to a boil. Add salt. Reduce heat to simmer and add the cornmeal in slow steady stream, stirring constantly. Continue cooking and stirring for 15 minutes. Add red bell pepper, fresh basil and parsley. Cook an additional 5 minutes, until polenta draws away from sides of pan.

Serves 4-6

Winter Warm-Up

1 gallon cider
12 to 15 whole cloves
½ stick cinnamon
1 t. powdered ginger
1 t. powdered nutmeg
orange twists, equal to skin of ½ to 1 orange

Simmer together 1 hour. Pour into mugs and top with twist of orange.

Serves 8-10

Italian Soda

Italian soda
whipped cream
fruit garnish

Fill a tall glass with ice and pour in your favorite Italian soda to within about an inch of the rim. Float whipped cream on top. Garnish with appropriate fruit to complement flavor of soda.

Baltimore Park Punch

orange, grapefruit and pineapple juice
grenadine
Orgeat syrup

Mix equal parts orange, grapefruit and pineapple juice with a dash of grenadine and Orgeat syrup. Blend well, and pour over ice in a tall glass. Garnish with a cherry and a pineapple spear.

Fresh Fruit Freezer

fresh fruit
crushed ice
sweet-and-sour mix
grenadine

To your selected fresh fruit, add equal part of crushed ice, sweet-and-sour mix and a dash of grenadine. Whir in blender. Garnish with fruit of choice.
There should be just enough liquid to cover ice in blender, so that the mix stays in frozen state and does not become liquid.

Coconut Pineapple Freeze

cream
sweet-and-sour mix
pineapple juice
coconut cream

Place equal parts cream, sweet-and-sour mix, pineapple juice and coconut cream into blender. Whirl until consistency of a Pina Colada.

Banana Fritters

6 whole eggs, separated
1 c. sugar
12 oz. beer
1 t. vanilla
flour to thicken
1 large banana, quartered

Beat egg yolks, sugar, beer and vanilla until smooth and blended. Add enough flour to thicken to heavy consistency. Fold in egg whites. Dip banana pieces into batter, covering completely and evenly.
Deep fry until golden brown on all sides.

Serves 4-6

Apple Torte

puff pastry
14 Granny Smith apples
1 jar apple jelly
2 T. cinnamon

1 12" fluted pan with drop-out bottom

Roll out puff pastry ½" thick and line pan with it. Peel apples and slice thin. Lay apples in pan in circular pattern. Pile apples high (they will cook down). Cook at 400 degrees until slightly brown and the apples are done through, about 15 minutes. Combine apple jelly and cinnamon in sauce pan, heat until liquefied. Pour over top of torte. Refrigerate.

Serves 6-8

70

NAPA VALLEY

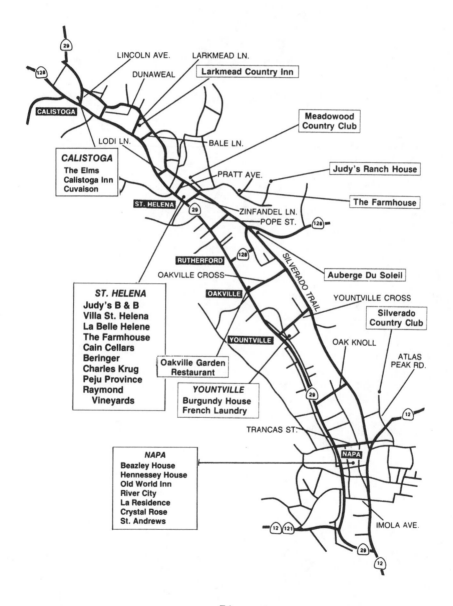

LINCOLN AVE.   LARKMEAD LN.

DUNAWEAL   **Larkmead Country Inn**

CALISTOGA

Meadowood Country Club

LODI LN.   BALE LN.

CALISTOGA
The Elms
Calistoga Inn
Cuvaison

PRATT AVE.

Judy's Ranch House

The Farmhouse

ST. HELENA   29   ZINFANDEL LN.
POPE ST.   128

RUTHERFORD   128

OAKVILLE CROSS

SILVERADO TRAIL

Auberge Du Soleil

ST. HELENA
Judy's B & B
Villa St. Helena
La Belle Helene
The Farmhouse
Cain Cellars
Beringer
Charles Krug
Peju Province
Raymond
  Vineyards

OAKVILLE

YOUNTVILLE CROSS

Silverado Country Club

YOUNTVILLE

OAK KNOLL

Oakville Garden
Restaurant

ATLAS
PEAK RD.

YOUNTVILLE
Burgundy House
French Laundry

29

TRANCAS ST.

12

NAPA
Beazley House
Hennessey House
Old World Inn
River City
La Residence
Crystal Rose
St. Andrews

NAPA

12 121

IMOLA AVE.

29

12

71

Beazley House

1910 First Street • Napa, California 94558
(707) 257-1649

Make new friends in Napa at the Beazley House. Carol and Jim Beazley, who are active in Napa Valley Bed & Breakfast Associations, have created a beautiful Inn from a landmark building, that maintains the charm of a quieter, more peaceful era. Sun streams through the stained glass windows in the entry way and casts muted colors on the inlaid, honey-toned oak floors of the music room. To the left is an inviting living room with a huge fireplace and a welcoming teacart set up with sherry, coffee and tea, to the right is the dining room where an ample Continental breakfast is served each morning. A reproduction of the mansion's carriage house is positioned at the rear of the property among gardens and manicured lawns. It contains four spacious rooms which reflect the "country" side of the Inn and each has its own cheery fireplace and private bath. The innkeepers also have copies of various menus from local restaurants and will happily make reservations and arrange winery tours, ballooning and a myriad of other activities for which the Napa Valley is famous.

73

Pumpkin or Banana Bread

1½ c. sugar
¾ c. oil
3 eggs
1½ c. canned pumpkin
3 c. unbleached flour
1½ t. baking powder
1½ t. baking soda
2 t. cinnamon
1 t. allspice
¼ t. cloves
1½ t. vanilla
¾ c. buttermilk
1 c. raisins
1 c. chopped almonds

Mix sugar, oil and eggs until fluffy; add pumpkin. Add 1½ c. of the flour, baking powder, soda and spices. Beat until smooth. Add the vanilla and buttermilk and beat again. Then add the remaining flour and beat until smooth. Add raisins and nuts and combine thoroughly. Pour mixture into a bundt pan and place in an oven preheated to 350 degrees for approximately 1 hour or until a toothpick comes out clean. Slice and serve warm. This bread freezes well and reheats in the microwave with little trouble. To make Banana Bread, omit the spices and raisins and substitute pureed bananas for the pumpkin.

Yield: 12 portions

Beazley House Muffins
(Cinnamon Crunch)

Dry Ingredients:

2 c. unbleached flour
⅓ c. sugar
2 t. baking powder
½ t. baking soda
½ c. chopped almonds

Wet Ingredients:

1 c. buttermilk
1 egg
⅓ c. oil

Topping Ingredients:

¼ c. sugar
1½ t. cinnamon

Mix dry ingredients together in a large bowl. In a separate container, mix wet ingredients thoroughly and pour into the dry, stirring just until the flour disappears. Batter should be lumpy. Do not over mix! Spray a muffin tin with a non-stick vegetable spray and spoon batter into the cups. Sprinkle each one with ½ t. of the sugar and cinnamon mixture. Bake at 400 degrees in a preheated oven for 15 to 20 minutes.

Yield: 1 dozen muffins

The Hennessey House
Bed and Breakfast Inn

1727 Main Street • Napa, California 94559
(707) 226-3774

Located in the Joseph Mathews Winery enclave and listed in the National Register of Historic Places, The Hennessey House combines the elegance of a bygone era with the conveniences of the 1980's. The stately residence and its companion carriage house were built in 1889 in the "East-Lake" style and have been painstakingly restored in an authentic Victorian motif. You can expect to spend a pampered night in one of the nine luxurious rooms, for each one has been tastefully decorated with antiques, lace curtains, queen size feather beds and private baths. In the morning awake refreshed and enjoy a hearty complimentary breakfast before setting out to explore convenient downtown Napa with its colorful array of specialty shops, galleries and restaurants.

77

Puffed Apple Walnut Pancake

6 eggs
1 c. flour
3 T. sugar
1 t. vanilla
½ t. salt
½ t. cinnamon
1 cube butter
2 apples, peeled and thinly sliced
¼ c. brown sugar
½ c. chopped walnuts

Preheat oven to 425 degrees. In blender mix first 6 ingredients until well blended. Melt the butter in a 13" x 9" baking dish in oven. Add apple slices and return to oven until butter sizzles. Remove from oven and immediately pour batter over apples. Mix brown sugar with nuts and sprinkle over batter. Bake 20 minutes or until pancake is puffed and brown. Serve immediately.

Serves 6-8

SILVERADO

Vintner's Court
and
Royal Oak

~~~~~~

1600 Atlas Peak Road • Napa, California 94558
(707) 257-0200
Hours: 6:00-10:00 p.m. Dinner, Wed., Thurs. and Sat.
6:00 p.m. and 9:00 p.m. seatings for Friday Seafood Buffet
10:00 a.m.-2:30 p.m. Sunday Brunch
Credit Cards: All Major
Prices: Expensive
Reservations: Recommended
Specialties: California Cuisine

~~~~~~

Among rows of pampered vines the Silverado Country Club stands in stately elegance and buried deep within its hallowed halls is a long-standing tradition with Napa Valley residents, The Vintner's Court Restaurant. Distinctive decor, exceptionally good food and attentive service are just a few of the reasons why this restaurant has become such an institution with locals. Another major reason is the Friday night Seafood Buffet, an extravaganza featuring the freshest seafood available in many taste-tempting preparations. There are two golf courses designed by Robert Trent Jones and 270 condominium units with a total of 450 rooms on the surrounding 1,200 acres. Tennis courts, a swimming pool and executive meeting facilities round out a total package and make any visit to the Silverado Country club one you'll never forget.

79

Grape Seed Oil and Basil Vinaigrette

1 c. grape seed oil
1 c. olive oil
1 c. red wine vinegar
⅓ c. honey
juice of 2 lemons
1 t. basil, chopped
1 t. chives, chopped
1 t. salt
1 t. white pepper
20 seedless grapes, cut in half

Place all ingredients in bowl and mix well. Serve over your favorite green salad.

Serves 8

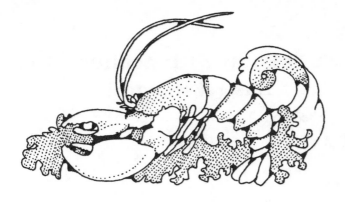

Seafood Pate

Preheat oven to 275 degrees.

½ lb. scallops
½ lb. Petrale sole
1 lb. fresh Maine lobster tail (meat only)
6 fresh or frozen prawns
4 egg whites
1 c. cream
½ c. white wine
1 t. chopped dill
6 spinach leaves, cooked
½ c. salmon eggs

Grind scallops, sole, lobster and prawns in a grinder. Place seafood mix in a blender, add all remaining ingredients except salmon eggs. Blend for 1 minute at medium speed, then place mixture in a bowl and fold in salmon eggs.

Place seafood mixture in loaf-shaped pan and cook it in a double boiler in oven for 1 hour. Test for doneness with toothpick. Slice and serve with sauce of your choice.

Serves 22

81

Fresh Salmon with Scallop Mousse

6 oz. fresh scallops, ground
4 prawns, ground
3 egg whites, whipped
½ c. heavy cream
2 t. salmon roe
salt to taste
white pepper to taste
fresh dill to taste
10 fresh spinach leaves
oil or butter
1 salmon filet, cut lengthwise into 2 thin slices
½ c. white wine
2 shallots, chopped
2 oz. butter
juice of half a lemon

Whip the scallops, prawns, egg whites, cream, salmon roe, salt, white pepper and dill well in a blender for about 10 seconds. Quickly saute the spinach leaves in a little oil or butter. Place spinach leaves on top of salmon slices; on top of leaves place scallop mousse; roll to form a roulade. Place in fish poacher or pan so that ends of the roulade are down and tucked under. Season salmon with salt and white pepper to taste, then poach salmon in the white wine, shallots, butter and lemon juice. Slice salmon into 4 pieces. Serve with a sauce, such as Dill, Hollandaise, Mousseline, Vin Blanc.

Serves 8 as an appetizer

Gravlaks Pacific Salmon

side of salmon, 8-10 lbs., boned, skin on
kosher salt
3 t. sugar
⅓ c. crushed black peppercorns
3 c. olive oil
1 c. fresh dill, chopped

Cover salmon completely with kosher salt, skin side down.
Refrigerate for 48 hours. Wipe off salt; sprinkle sugar over salmon
and press peppercorns into salmon. Pour olive oil over fish, then
sprinkle with dill. Refrigerate for 48 hours. Slice and serve.

Serves 25

Pit Roasted Elk
Over Mesquite Charcoal

3 lbs. boneless elk loin
3 fresh bay leaves
⅓ bunch fresh oregano
⅓ bunch fresh thyme
20 juniper berries
2 c. port wine
1 c. olive oil
1 oz. walnut oil
⅓ c. wine vinegar
salt
cracked black pepper

Marinate elk in first 9 ingredients for 48 hours. Cook over mesquite, season with salt and cracked black pepper. Brush meat 2 or 3 times with marinade while cooking. When meat is cooked to your liking, slice and serve.

Serves 6

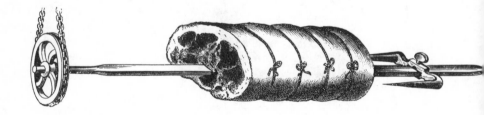

BED AND
BREAKFAST

The Old World Inn

1301 Jefferson Street • Napa, California 94559
(707) 257-0112

The Old World Inn lives up to its name. Light and airy Victorian themes with old-fashioned hospitality invite guests to relax and renew themselves. The grand old residence is gloriously decorated with exquisite antique Victorian furnishings. Each piece has been carefully selected to match a vibrant color scheme inspired by renowned Swedish artist Carl Larsson. Quaint old axioms are hand-stenciled above the doorways and upper portions of the high-ceilinged morning room where a beautifully presented Continental breakfast is served. The wonderful rooms are individually decorated with matching linens, and each has its own private bathroom. A freeform, custom Jacuzzi will help soak out the kinks before setting off for a fun filled evening in Napa. Stop by for a visit and you'll want to return to this charming Bed and Breakfast Inn over and over.

85

Desperately Healthy Pancakes

½ c. soy flour
½ c. whole wheat flour
½ c. unbleached all-purpose flour
2 T. wheat germ
2 T. powdered milk
2 T. unprocessed bran
1 T. baking powder
½ t. baking soda
¼ t. salt
grated peel of 1 orange

Mix together the above 10 ingredients.

2 eggs, separated
½ c. plain yogurt
¼ c. oil
1 T. molasses
1 T. honey
1½ c. orange juice

Add egg yolks, yogurt, oil, molasses, honey and orange juice to flour mixture; blend well. Beat egg whites until stiff. Fold into pancake mixture. Cook on 300 degree griddle. Cook 2½ minutes one side and 1 minute on the other. Look for nice hollow bubbles on first cooking.

Makes about 36 3" cakes

Orange Pancake Syrup

2 T. water
¾ c. brown sugar
½ c. orange concentrate
¼ lb. butter
1 t. maple flavoring or 2 T. maple syrup
4 T. orange peel, grated
½ c. honey

Boil water, brown sugar and orange concentrate together. In processor bowl blend together butter, maple flavoring (or syrup) and orange peel. Add the sugar-orange mixture. Blend well. Blend in honey. Serve over pancakes, waffles or French toast.

Amaretto Torte

Preheat oven to 325 degrees. Grease three 3" x 8" layer tins.

2 c. sugar
½ c. margarine
½ c. mayonnaise
½ c. Wesson oil
2 eggs
½ c. cocoa

Amaretto Torte (con't)

1 c. buttermilk
½ t. salt
2 t. vanilla
2 t. baking soda
2¾ c. all-purpose flour
1 c. boiling water
½ c. Amaretto
chocolate icing (recipe follows)
half walnuts

Cream together sugar and margarine, and add mayonnaise and oil. Add eggs. Beat well. Add cocoa and slowly add buttermilk. Add remaining ingredients.
Mix well. Add 1 c. boiling water. Fill 3 cake tins equally. Bake 35 minutes at 325 degrees or until done. Remove from pans and cool. Wrap in Saran wrap and freeze until ready to use.
Remove from freezer and slice frozen tortes in half. Sprinkle ½ c. Amaretto equally on both halves. Spread chocolate icing on cut side of bottom half, and replace top half. Spread chocolate icing on top of cakes and decorate with half walnuts.

Makes 3 tortes

Chocolate Icing

1 pint heavy whipping cream
20 oz. good quality cooking chocolate (we use Guittard
    Chocolate Drops)

In pan, bring cream to a boil. Remove from heat and stir in chocolate. Stir until smooth icing forms (this can be done in a food processor). This icing will keep in a refrigerator for a month or more.

88

La Residence
COUNTRY INN

4066 St. Helena Highway • Napa, California 94558
(707) 253-0337

Sheltered by the rolling green foothills of majestic Mt. St. Helena, in the picturesque village of St. Helena, La Residence Country Inn takes guests back to a less complicated era. The grand mansion and its companion, a French style barn named Cabernet Hall, have a total of fifteen rooms, all with private baths and some also have patios or balconies. Enjoy a Continental breakfast in front of a cheery fireplace in the dining room and a wine hour hosted by your innkeepers in the afternoon. Don't forget your swimsuit. A hot tub and Jacuzzi are available for guests and a pool is now under construction.

89

Pumpkin Roll

3 eggs
1 c. white sugar
⅔ c. pumpkin
1 t. lemon juice
¾ c. flour
1 t. baking powder
½ t. salt
2 t. cinnamon
1 t. ginger
1 t. nutmeg
powdered sugar

Filling:

1 c. powdered sugar
1 T. butter
6 oz. cream cheese
½ t. vanilla
1 c. chopped walnuts
garnish: whole walnuts

Beat eggs for 5 minutes at high speed. Gradually add the sugar. Stir in pumpkin and lemon juice. Sift together flour, baking powder, salt, cinnamon, ginger and nutmeg. Fold into pumpkin mixture. Spread into 15" x 10" x 1" pan lined with greased and floured foil. Bake at 375 degrees for 15 minutes or until light brown. Turn out on towel covered with powdered sugar. Starting at narrow end, roll towel and cake together. Cool, then unroll.
Filling: Beat powdered sugar, butter, cream cheese and vanilla until smooth. Fold in walnuts and spread over cake, reserving a little for the top. Roll cake up, garnish with reserved filling and whole walnuts and slice like jelly roll.

Serves 10

NAPA, CA   LA RESIDENCE COUNTRY INN

Spritz Ribbon Cookies

½ c. butter
½ c. powdered sugar
½ t. almond extract
1 egg yolk, beaten
1¼ c. cake flour
¼ t. salt

Preheat oven to 400 degrees. Cream butter. Add powdered sugar, beat well until soft and creamy. Add almond extract and egg yolk. Gradually stir in sifted flour and salt. Put dough into cookie press using the ribbon nozzle form. Press out onto floured surface, cut into 5" strips, and bake on ungreased sheet for approximately 8 minutes or until brown around the edge of cookie.

Makes approximately 24 cookies

Brandy Alexander

½ gallon vanilla ice cream
½ c. brandy

Soften ice cream. Mix the softened ice cream and the brandy in a heavy duty mixer or food processor. Return mixture to freezer in stainless steel bowl or plastic container with lid. Freeze for 24 hours. Serve in a champagne saucer.

Serves 6

SAUVIGNON BLANC

NAPA VALLEY

PRODUCED AND BOTTLED BY PEJU PROVINCE
OAKVILLE, CALIFORNIA • ALCOHOL 12.0% BY VOLUME

An absolutely delightful Sauvignon Blanc made nearly
perfect by the addition of just 20% Semillon which tones down
the Sauvignon's proverbial grassiness.

Pairs perfectly with seafood and fowl.

505 Lincoln Avenue • Napa, California 94558
(707) 253-1111
Hours: 11:30 a.m.-2:30 p.m. Lunch, Mon.-Fri.
5:00-10:00 p.m. Dinner, Seven days a week
Bar is open 10:00 a.m.-12:00 p.m. weekdays;
11:00 p.m.-1:00 a.m. weekends
Credit Cards: Am. Express, Visa, M/C
Reservations: Suggested
Specialties: American Cuisine

"I loved it" is what you'll tell your friends after a visit to River City in Napa. One of the partners, Candy Barazi, likes to say River City serves "a good meal at an honest price in a comfortable atmosphere." It's true. Muted colors in the carpet and creamy beige walls set off dark blue booths, grey-caned captains' chairs and lively wine prints. A large picture window overlooks the lovely Napa River. The diverse menu presents a difficult decision, so come hungry, because you'll want to try everything!

Hearts of Palm Salad

2 hearts of palm, sliced in rounds
½ red bell pepper, julienne cut
2 anchovies, chopped
3 oz. tarragon dressing (recipe follows)
mixed greens—
american endive, chopped fine
red leaf lettuce, torn bite size
romaine, chopped
watercress, leaves only
sorrel leaves, torn

Toss all ingredients together lightly. Serve in chilled bowls.

Serves 2

Tarragon Dressing

1 egg yolk
4 cloves garlic, chopped
2 T. Dijon mustard
2 c. salad oil
2 t. tarragon, sauteed in ¼ c. white vinegar
½ c. fresh lemon juice
salt to taste

Lightly whisk egg yolk, garlic and mustard. Add oil in slow, steady stream, whisking constantly, until all oil is incorporated. Add sauteed tarragon, then lemon juice until mixed. Salt to taste. Refrigerate.

Chicken Breast Stuffed with Julienne Vegetables in Basil Cream Sauce

6 whole chicken breasts, boned and skinned
salt and pepper
½ c. banana squash, julienne cut
½ c. zucchini, julienne cut
½ c. red bell pepper, julienne cut
½ c. green bell pepper, julienne cut
½ c. jicama, julienne cut
1 c. dry white wine
1 c. water

Pound chicken breasts lightly on inside. Sprinkle with salt and pepper. Divide vegetables among the 6 breasts, laying the julienne strips across the center seam of the breast. Fold the breast over the vegetables and roll, overlapping the ends. Place close together, seam side down, in a shallow baking pan. Pour in 1 c. dry white wine and 1 c. water. Cover with aluminum foil. Bake 15-20 minutes, until breast is tender.

To serve: Place Basil Cream Sauce (recipe follows) on plate; then place chicken on sauce. Put a spoonful of sauce over the center of the rolled breast. Garnish with a strip of red bell pepper.

Serves 6

Basil Cream Sauce

½ c. butter
2 c. heavy cream
¼ c. pesto*

Melt butter in saucepan. Whisk in cream in a slow, steady stream, over medium heat until it is incorporated into butter. Add pesto, whisk until mixed.
*See Glossary

95

Walnut Pecan Torte

Crust:

1⅓ c. white flour
¼ c. sweet butter, cold
2 T. white sugar
1 egg
1 egg white to seal pastry

Filling:

¾ c. white sugar
¼ c. light corn syrup
2 T. Kahlua
⅓ c. heavy cream
1½ c. walnut halves
1½ c. pecan halves

Mix thoroughly; let stand 30 minutes while preparing crust.

Blend flour, butter and sugar in food processor until fine crumbs are formed. Add 1 egg. Blend in food processor until dough adheres together.

Press crust dough to line a 10" removable bottom tart pan. Make sure there are no seams open at edges. Brush crust with egg white to seal. Place on sheet pan. Pour in filling. Bake in 350 degree oven for 35 to 45 minutes. Filling will bubble as it cooks and become caramelized. Cover edges with foil to prevent over browning. Cool. Remove from tart pan. Cut into 10 pieces and serve with whipped heavy cream and a nut garnish.

Serves 10

THE FRENCH LAUNDRY

6640 Washington Street • Yountville, California 94599
(707) 944-2380
Hours: One seating Wed. through Sun.
Credit Cards: None
Prices: Expensive
Reservations: Only
Specialties: Eclectic

Make reservations early for dinner at The French Laundry, the charming French country restaurant where guests are allowed complete freedom to wander through the gardens or visit the kitchen for a chat with the chef as she prepares the evening's prix fixe menu. Baskets of fresh fruit, flowers and the soft glow of the firelight and flickering candles lend romance and create a relaxed atmosphere. The ever-changing menu could start with Smoked Trout, Curried Chicken Mousse with Cantaloupe and Chutney or Pate of Poussin Livers. Next, maybe, a creamy Broccoli Soup with Ginger and Garlic followed, perhaps, by an entree of Normandy Pork with Apples and Onions, Duckling with Green Peppercorn Sauce, Veal and Chantrelles with Rosemary and Orange or a fantastic Supreme of Chicken in Lemon and Mint. If possible, try a wonderful piece of Apple Kuchen with Hot Cream Sauce, Fig and Chocolate Chantilly or a light and soothing Pomegranate Sorbet. No matter what you choose at The French Laundry, expect the best.

97

Broccoli Soup
with Ginger and Garlic

2 medium potatoes, peeled and sliced
2 c. water, or 2 c. chicken stock and water combined
salt and pepper
2 T. ginger, finely chopped
2 T. garlic, finely chopped
4 T. butter
1 bunch broccoli, sliced thin (use all stems)
2 c. light cream

Cover potatoes with water and/or stock, add salt and pepper to taste, cover and bring to a fast boil. Reduce heat and cook until very tender, about 20 minutes. While they are cooking, gently saute ginger and garlic in butter until golden; set aside. When potatoes are tender, replace water if necessary, return to a boil and add the broccoli. Cover and cook 2-3 minutes or just until tender, add ginger and garlic mixture, and puree in the blender immediately. Add cream, and correct salt and pepper if necessary. A few nice broccoli leaves may be saved and slivered for a garnish.

Serves 6

Shrimp in Beer
with Red Pepper Sauce

For Sauce:

6 red bell peppers
1 small onion, minced
2 cloves garlic, minced
2 T. olive oil
2 T. butter
1 c. chicken stock
1 small hot red pepper
salt and pepper

18 large shrimp
2 bottles beer (light)
2 T. butter

Make the sauce first. Char the red bell peppers over a gas flame or under the broiler. Put into a paper bag to steam for a few minutes, then rub off the blackened peel and rinse briefly. Chop coarsely after removing seeds (reserve ½ pepper to cut into a fine chiffonade for garnish). Saute onion and garlic gently in olive oil and butter. Add the red bell pepper, stock and the hot pepper. Let simmer for 15 minutes. Season with salt and pepper to taste, and puree mixture in blender. Set aside in a pan to reheat before serving time. Peel shrimp. Heat beer and butter to a simmer. When ready to serve, add the shrimp and simmer just until they curl and turn opaque. Put a generous spoonful of the heated sauce on a heated plate, arrange 3 shrimp on top, and garnish with the chiffonade of red bell pepper.

Serves 6

Braised Oxtails

½ c. flour
salt and black pepper
3-4 whole oxtails, approximately 6 lbs., cut between joints
olive oil
3 large or 4 medium onions, cut lengthwise into chunks
4 cloves garlic, sliced
1 c. red wine
1 c. beef or chicken stock
1 orange, sliced into quarter slices

Put flour, and salt and pepper to taste into a paper bag; add oxtail
pieces and shake well to coat. Shake off excess flour and brown
the pieces well in olive oil. Remove oxtails to a casserole, then
brown the onion and garlic. Stir in the wine and stock. Bring
to a boil. Distribute the orange slices over the oxtails and pour
the hot onion and stock mixture over them. Add more pepper
and salt if you feel it needs more.

Cover and cook for about 4 hours in a slow oven (325 degrees).
When very tender, pour all juices off into a large glass measuring
cup. This makes it easy to skim off the fat. Taste juices for seasoning, add more salt and pepper if needed, and pour back over the
oxtails. Serve with rice or a simple pasta. Garnish with lots of
chopped parsley and a little orange zest.

Serves 6

Pumpkin Cream Cheese Torte

Crust:

½ package zwieback
5 Amaretti cookies
⅓ c. sugar
¾ to 1 cube butter, melted

Crush zwieback and cookies. Mix with sugar. Add butter gradually until mixture will stick together when pressed between fingers. Press into removable bottom 10" torte pan or pie plate. Bake 15 minutes at 350 degrees. Cool.

Filling:

1 envelope gelatin
¼ c. cold water
about ½ c. brandy
1 c. brown sugar, loosely filled
¼ t. nutmeg
¼ t. powdered ginger (be generous)
½ t. cinnamon
10 oz. natural cream cheese (Philadelphia Brand is okay if
   natural is unavailable)
1½ c. whipping cream
1½-2 c. pumpkin
whipped cream and toasted almonds or toasted coconut
   for garnish

Soften gelatin in cold water in a measuring cup. Set cup into a water bath and heat until gelatin is thoroughly dissolved. Add brandy to the ⅔ c. line.

Mix brown sugar, nutmeg, ginger and cinnamon. Pour gelatin

Pumpkin Cream Cheese Torte (con't)

mixture into sugar mixture, and stir until smooth to dissolve the sugar and cool down the gelatin mixture. You may need to strain it to remove lumps.

In mixer, beat the cream cheese until soft and smooth. Gradually add whipping cream, using spatula to make sure cream cheese is all incorporated. Continue beating until mixture is like soft whipped cream, then slowly drizzle in the gelatin/sugar mixture while beating on low speed. Add pumpkin with beater on low. Remove beaters, fold by hand to make sure it is all mixed from bottom.

Spoon into shell and chill. Top with whipped cream and garnish with the almonds or coconut.

Makes 1 torte

Burgundy House
Bordeaux House
Country Inns

σσσσσσσσσσσσσσσσσσσ

6711 Washington Street • Yountville, California 94599
(707) 944-2855

σσσσσσσσσσσσσσσσσσσ

Three stars for the Burgundy House and its more formal twin, the Bordeaux. These classic Bed and Breakfast Inns have been labeled "the most luxurious of the valley's inns." The Burgundy House was erected in the 1870's from hand-hewn fieldstone, and its walls are a cool twenty two inches thick. The neighboring Bordeaux House is an impressive red brick Inn reminiscent of the famous Bordeaux region of France. The Burgundy House has six rooms done in a French country-inn motif with fireplaces and distinctive furnishings. The more elegant Bordeaux House boasts gracious accommodations. Each of its six rooms also has fireplaces and individual patios to enjoy the spectacular views of this incomparable valley. A wonderful breakfast is included in the price of the room.

103

Val's Slumgolian

1 lb. hamburger
1 large onion
1 garlic clove, minced
1 can sliced mushrooms, or equal amount of fresh
   mushrooms, sliced
1 bell pepper, chopped
4 15 oz. cans tomato sauce
1 small can tomato paste
1 can corn
1 can black olives
parsley
basil
oregano
1 package wide egg noodles

Brown hamburger, drain and add onion, garlic, mushrooms, bell
pepper, tomato sauce, tomato paste, corn, olives and herbs (to
taste). Simmer sauce. Cook and drain noodles; toss with the hot
sauce.

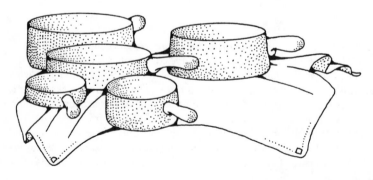

Burgundy House Fruit Plate

For winter fruits

bananas
lemon juice
almonds, sliced or walnuts, ground
apples
Fruit Fresh *or*
vitamin C powder
cinnamon
sugar
oranges
coconut
grapefruit
powdered sugar
fresh mint, if available

Slice bananas, dip in lemon juice, sprinkle with sliced almonds
or ground walnuts. Slice apples, dip in Fruit Fresh or vitamin C
powder and water (to keep from turning brown). Sprinkle with
cinnamon and sugar. Slice oranges, sprinkle with coconut. Slice
grapefruit, sprinkle with powdered sugar. Arrange on tray.
Garnish with fresh mint or other greens.

Grandma Keenan's Scotch Nut Bread

1 egg
1 c. sugar
2 c. milk
2 scant c. white flour
2 scant c. whole wheat flour
½ t. salt
1 t. baking powder

Grandma Keenan's Scotch Nut Bread (con't)

1 t. soda
1 t. maple flavoring
1 scant c. raisins
1 c. nuts, chopped

Mix ingredients well. Pour into two greased loaf pans. Let rise in pans 30 minutes. Bake at 350 degrees for 45 minutes to 1 hour, or until it tests done (when toothpick inserted into center comes out clean).

Yield: 2 loaves

Lemon Jello Cake
by Aunt Edith

Cake:

4 eggs
¾ c. corn oil
¾ c. water
1 package lemon Jello
1 package Betty Crocker Yellow Cake mix

Beat eggs well. Add corn oil, water and powdered Jello. Beat well. Add cake mix. Bake at 325-350 degrees in a long Pyrex cake dish 35-40 minutes. Glaze while hot.

Lemon Glaze:

1½ c. powdered sugar
lemon juice
lemon rind

Mix powdered sugar and lemon juice to make a thin icing. Add grated lemon rind. Spread on cake while hot. (Use more sugar and lemon juice as you wish.)

Orange or Bleu Cheese Biscuits

Orange:

1 package Pillsbury Biscuit mix
sugar cubes
frozen orange juice concentrate

Soak sugar cube in orange juice concentrate and place in middle of biscuit. Bake as directed. Good for breakfast!

Bleu Cheese:

1 package Pillsbury Biscuit mix
1 small package bleu cheese

Place chunk of bleu cheese in middle of biscuit and bake as directed. Easy!

Crystal
Rose Inn

Bed & Breakfast
Napa Valley

7564 St. Helena Highway • Napa, California 94558
(707) 944-8185

The homey and quiet Crystal Rose Inn offers a welcome escape from daily pressures in a charming Queen Anne Victorian Bed and Breakfast Inn. There are three comfortable rooms with private baths, all tastefully decorated with antiques and little touches that make visiting this Inn such a pleasure. Stroll through groomed gardens or relax on the porch and enjoy a glass of wine while you choose a restaurant from the many sample menus that are available in the cozy parlor. A complimentary breakfast of freshly baked breads, muffins with homemade jams, coffee and juice is served each morning.

109

Banana Nut Bread

1 c. sugar
2 T. soft shortening
1 egg
¾ c. milk
1 c. mashed bananas
3 c. flour
3½ t. baking powder
1 t. salt
¾ c. chopped nuts

Mix sugar, shortening and egg thoroughly. Stir in milk and banana. Sift together flour, baking powder and salt. Add to liquid ingredients, stirring until dry ingredients are moistened. Blend in chopped nuts.
Pour into well greased 9" x 5" x 3" loaf pan. Let stand 20 minutes before baking. Bake at 350 degrees 70 minutes, until toothpick comes out clean.

Yield: 1 loaf

Pumpkin Bread

1 c. brown sugar
½ c. sugar
1½ c. canned pumpkin
½ c. salad oil
2 eggs
2 c. flour
1 t. soda

Pumpkin Bread (con't)

½ t. each salt, nutmeg, cinnamon
¼ t. ginger
1 c. raisins
½ c. chopped nuts
¼ c. water

Combine sugars, pumpkin, oil and eggs; beat until well blended. Sift together flour, soda, salt and spices. Add to pumpkin mix and mix well. Stir in raisins, nuts and water. Spoon into well oiled 9" x 5" x 3" loaf pan. Bake at 350 degrees for 65 to 75 minutes, or until done when tested. Turn out on rack to cool.

Serves 12

Zucchini Bread

3 eggs
1 c. oil
2 c. sugar
2 c. grated raw zucchini
2 c. sifted flour
¼ t. baking powder
2 t. baking soda
1 t. salt
3 t. cinnamon
3 t. vanilla
1 c. chopped nuts

Beat eggs; add oil, sugar and zucchini. Sift dry ingredients and add to mixture. Add vanilla and nuts. Grease and flour 2 loaf pans. Pour into pans and bake 1 hour at 350 degrees.

Yield: 2 loaves

OAKVILLE

garden

RESTAURANT

7848 Highway 29 • Oakville, California 94562
(707) 944-8016
Hours: 11:30 a.m.-3:00 p.m. Lunch, every day except Wed.
5:30-10:00 p.m. Dinner, Thurs.-Sun.
10:00 a.m.-3:00 p.m. Brunch, Sat. & Sun.
Credit Cards: M/C, Visa, Diner's Club
Reservations: Suggested
Specialties: California and French

Emerald vineyards surround the cozy Oakville Garden Restaurant where generous portions of delicious California and French cuisine are served with a smile. Dine on the patio, in the fragrant garden, or inside the lovely dining room. Incredibly fresh produce, some from their own garden, tasteful presentation and quality meats and seafood provide the basis for a constantly changing menu. Daily blackboard specials and exciting entrees with unusual treatments pique the interest of even the most jaded gourmet. One visit should convince you to make this jewel of a restaurant a regular haunt.

Prawns Provencal

½ T. butter
½ T. olive oil
20 large prawns
2 T. chopped shallots
2 T. chopped garlic
2 oz. brandy
1 c. white wine
¼ c. fumet*
1 T. capers
3 T. chopped parsley (preferably flat leaf variety)
juice of 2 lemons
2 T. tomato, diced and seeded
salt to taste
4 oz. unsalted butter

Melt butter in frying pan and add olive oil. Saute prawns in two batches over high heat until just pink outside; remove from pan. Wipe pan clear, add shallots and sweat until soft. Add garlic, stir until fragrant. Deglaze pan with brandy and add white wine and fumet. Cook over high heat until liquids are reduced by half. Add capers, parsley, lemon juice and tomato. Add salt if necessary, reduce to simmer and add butter piece by piece, stirring constantly until sauce is smooth. Add prawns and cook until heated throughout.

Serves 4

*See Glossary

Snails in Wild Mushrooms and Madeira

Oil
32 large snails (preferably French)
4 T. chopped shallots
4 oz. wild mushrooms (Oriental forest/shitake/chanterelle or whatever else is available)
2 oz. brandy
6 oz. Madeira
4 oz. fumet*
⅓ c. chopped parsley
salt and pepper to taste
1 c. heavy cream

Heat a large heavy pan. Add just enough oil to lightly cover bottom of pan. Add snails and shallots, cook 1 minute. Add mushrooms and continue to cook 1 minute longer.

Remove pan from flame, add brandy, return pan to flame. When most of the liquids are evaporated add Madeira and fumet. Cook until reduced by half. Add parsley, salt and pepper to taste and cream. Continue to cook until sauce has reduced enough to heavily coat spoon.

Serves 8

*See Glossary

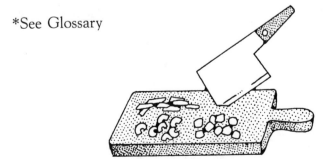

115

180 Rutherford Road • Rutherford, California 94573
(707) 963-1211

Sheltered by a thirty three acre olive grove, the impressive Auberge Du Soleil Restaurant and Inn awaits couples seeking a romantic weekend of pampering and luxury, or a retreat for executives where every demand has been anticipated by a courteous and efficient staff. The maisons were recently built to accompany the critically acclaimed restaurant and each one is stocked with cheese, wine, fruit trays and professionally decorated to embody comfort and elegance. A host of activities can be arranged through the Inn, from leisurely picnics in discreet settings, elegantly catered parties and seminars, or ballooning, wine tours, golf and glider rides. All within easy driving distance of the beautiful Auberge Du Soleil.

117

ESTATE BOTTLED

Beringer.

CHARDONNAY
NAPA VALLEY

GROWN, PRODUCED AND
BOTTLED BY BERINGER
VINEYARDS B.W. 46

ST. HELENA, CALIFORNIA
ALCOHOL 13.3% BY VOL.
750 ML

This Chardonnay is lush and rich with a slight toastiness
which adds complexity to intense-citrus-like fruit flavors.

Food Pairings: Firm acidity and high fruit levels make for an
excellent match with full-flavored seafoods such as salmon, bass
or shellfish. Cream based sauces utilizing veal stocks and any
citrus flavored sauces will pair tastily with this wine.

Tuna With Black Pepper

4-6 oz. portions of Ahi tuna
salt and cracked pepper
2 oz. butter
2 oz. cognac
6 oz. reduced veal stock
4 oz. cream

Salt tuna steak and season with salt and black pepper to taste. Saute in hot butter for 5 minutes on each side. Flambe with cognac, and put tuna aside.

Add veal stock and cream. Reduce until mixture thickens. Serve immediately with fresh pasta.

Serves 1

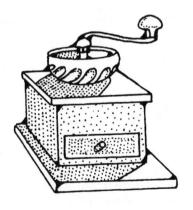

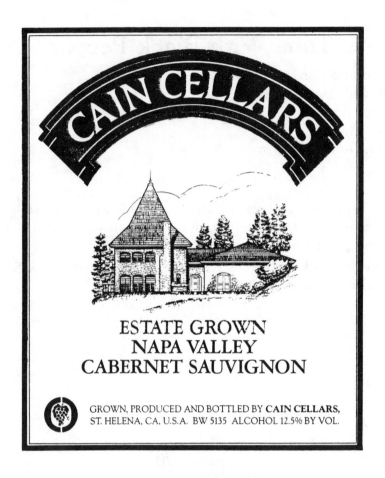

ESTATE GROWN
NAPA VALLEY
CABERNET SAUVIGNON

GROWN, PRODUCED AND BOTTLED BY **CAIN CELLARS,**
ST. HELENA, CA, U.S.A. BW 5135 ALCOHOL 12.5% BY VOL.

Mingled aromas of oak and fruit, vanilla, cedar, cherries and black pepper are all combined in an elegant, balanced wine. Enjoyable now, it will improve for a decade.

This is an outstanding wine to accompany a wide range of flavorful meat dishes.

120

Wine Sorbet

10 oz. cool water
7 oz. Cabernet Sauvignon or Sauvignon Blanc wine jelly

Whisk together the cool water and the jelly in a bowl until the jelly is completely dissolved and the solution is clear.

Pour the mixture into an ice cream maker and allow the machine to process the mixture until the sorbet begins to form. Allow 25 to 35 minutes. Test for desired consistency.

Wine Jelly Sweet & Sour Sauce

⅓ c. cider vinegar
⅓ c. Cabernet Sauvignon wine jelly
2 T. cornstarch
3 T. soy sauce
⅓ c. water
4 oz. cooked meat
¼ c. sesame seed (optional)

Mix vinegar, jelly, cornstarch, soy sauce and water together in a wok over medium heat.

Stir continuously until mixture thickens. Add cooked meat and mix lightly until evenly coated. Add ¼ c. sesame seeds if desired and stir lightly to coat.

Baked Cabernet Brie

Desired amount of Brie
Desired amount of Cabernet Sauvignon wine jelly
Puff pastry

Spread the Cabernet Sauvignon wine jelly over the Brie. Wrap the Brie in puff pastry and bake at 450 degrees until golden brown. Serve immediately.

LA BELLE HELENE RESTAURANT

―――――――――――

∽∾∽∾∽∾∽∾∽∾∽∾∽∾∽∾∽∾∽∾∽

1345 Railroad Road • St. Helena, California 94574
(707) 963-1234
Hours: 6:00-9:30 p.m. Dinner, Mon., Tues., Thurs.,
Fri. & Sat., Closed Wednesdays
Credit Cards: Visa, M/C
Prices: Expensive
Specialties: French

∽∾∽∾∽∾∽∾∽∾∽∾∽∾∽∾∽∾∽∾∽

Unpretentious elegance reigns at La Belle Helene. Hushed conversation blends with the soft tinkle of a piano to create intimate dining with more than a hint of romance. Fresh flowers and unusual palette-knife art work add splashes of color to the backdrop of stone walls. Meanwhile, behind the scenes in the kitchen, Chef Marc is busy creating succulent dishes, such as Breast of Muscovie Duck with Papaya Sauce, Loin of Pork with Five Peppercorn Sauce, Venision Loin with Walnut Sauce and a Chestnut tartlet and Filet of Beef with Pine Nuts, Roquefort and Shallot Sauce. There is much, much more but mere words do an injustice—experience La Belle Helene and see if you don't agree.

123

Scallop and Saffron Soup

¼ c. olive oil
2 oz. butter
½ onion, coarsely chopped
2 shallots, coarsely chopped
2 cloves garlic, coarsely chopped
½ leek, washed and coarsely chopped
1 celery rib, washed and coarsely chopped
1 sprig parsley, coarsely chopped
½ t. fennel seed
½ t. whole white pepper, crushed
dash of cayenne pepper
½ t. coriander, crushed
1 sprig fresh thyme, leaves only
1 bay leaf
1 c. white wine (dry Sauvignon Blanc)
6 c. strong fish stock
1½ oz. saffron
1 pt. heavy cream
2½ lbs. fresh scallops*
½ loaf French bread
½ lb. butter, melted
¼ lb. coarsely grated parmesan cheese
finely chopped fresh chives

In a large pan, heat olive oil and butter together. Add next 12 ingredients and cook until ingredients are translucent. Add white wine, reduce by ¾, add fish stock and cook for 20-25 minutes. Strain liquid into another pan through a fine sieve. Add saffron and cream. Reduce again until soup starts to thicken. (Soup should be spicy—adjust seasonings if necessary.) Add scallops* and poach for about 5 minutes at a very slow simmer. To prepare croutons, slice bread into 20 thin slices and place them on a baking sheet. Brush lightly with melted butter and sprinkle parmesan cheese

Scallop and Saffron Soup (con't)

over them. Bake in an oven, preheated at 375 degrees, until nicely browned, crispy and dry. Serve soup immediately and place 2 croutons on top of each bowl. Sprinkle with fresh chives.

Serves 8-10

*Note: Scallops may be replaced by clams or mussels and are to be treated the same way.

Pommes de Terre Paillasson
(Marc's Potato Pancake)

6 potatoes, peeled (Idaho preferably)
4 cloves garlic, peeled and smashed
2 shallots, finely minced
4 sprigs parsley, finely chopped
salt and pepper
1 c. oil
3 T. butter

Grate potatoes coarsely. Take ½ c. of potatoes in your hands and press them to remove all excess liquid. Repeat until all grated potatoes are used.

Place potatoes in a mixing bowl and add garlic, shallots and parsley. Season with salt and pepper to taste and mix thoroughly.

At this time, the potatoes can be made individually in small pancakes or in a bigger pan and then cut like a pie. The principle and the technique remain the same.

Heat the oil in a saute pan (non-stick) on high heat. When the oil becomes smoky, place potatoes in the pan and using a spatula, press the potatoes until they cover the entire bottom of the pan with even thickness. Cook them for approximately 10-15 minutes and flip them on the other side. Add butter and place the pan in a preheated oven at 375 degrees until potatoes are crisp and cooked.

Serves 6-8

Roasted Venison Loin with Walnut Sauce and Apple Stuffed with Raspberries

2 T. oil
1 lb. venison scraps (trimmings)
1 oz. crushed black pepper
1 carrot, coarsely chopped
1 onion, coarsely chopped
2 shallots, coarsely chopped
2 cloves garlic, coarsely chopped
6 juniper berries, crushed
1 sprig thyme
1 bay leaf
1 c. port wine
3 c. strong veal or venison stock
10 apples
5 oz. butter
5 oz. sugar
2¼ lb. (approx.) venison loin, tied firmly
¼ c. crushed black pepper
1 T. oil
2 c. fresh walnuts
½ c. brandy
1 c. heavy cream
50 raspberries

Preheat oven to 475 degrees. In a saucepan, over high heat, bring 2 T. of oil to "smoky", add venison scraps and crushed black pepper. Cook until brown. Add carrot, onion, shallots, garlic, juniper berries, thyme and bay leaf. Cook for about 15-20 minutes, reducing heat to medium. Add port wine and reduce by ¼. Add stock, bring to a boil and reduce by ½ (skimming top of sauce as it reduces).

Roasted Venison Loin (con't)

Meanwhile, cut top of each apple and scoop out core. Place half an ounce of butter and half an ounce of sugar in the core cavity. Place each apple on a baking sheet and bake for approximately 15-20 minutes, or until fruit gets slightly soft. Reserve in warm place until serving.

Roll venison loin in crushed black pepper, making sure to spread it evenly all around surface of meat and lightly sprinkle with salt. In an oven-proof skillet over high heat, bring 1 T. of oil to "smoky". Brown each side of the loin and bake in oven at 475 degrees for about 30 minutes for rare/medium; 20 minutes for rare.

While the loin is roasting, in another saucepan, place walnuts and brandy together and reduce to almost dry. (Be cautious, the brandy will ignite when it reaches a certain heat). Strain the stock reduction through a fine sieve onto the walnut pan and add heavy cream. Reduce until desired consistency and quantity; adjust seasonings just before serving.

To serve, place one ladle of sauce on each 12" plate. Thinly slice the venison loin and place on each plate evenly (you should fan out each slice around the edge of the plate). Stuff each apple with 5 raspberries, replace cap about each apple and place 1 per plate. Garnish with watercress and serve.

Serves 10

Chef's Note: Fresh pasta, potato pancake or polenta would be a good accompaniment.

127

Les Profiterolles au Chocolat

1 pint of water or milk
½ lb. butter, unsalted
¼ t. salt
2 oz. sugar
10 oz. flour, sifted
8 eggs (+ 1 for eggwash)
1 pint vanilla ice cream

Over low heat add the water or milk, butter, salt and sugar. When the milk boils, add flour and mix with a wooden spatula, cook for about 5 minutes over low heat. Place mixture in mixing bowl and whip at low speed. Gradually add the whole eggs until the mixture has completely absorbed them. Pipe 24 choux paste* onto a baking sheet lined with waxed paper. Lightly egg wash each "choux" and bake them at 475 degrees for approximately 35-40 minutes (the last 5 minutes of baking the door of the oven should remain ajar to let out the humidity produced by the cream puff).

Slice each cream puff in half; stuff them with vanilla ice cream, and cover them with hot chocolate sauce (recipe follows), placing 3 per plate. Whipped cream and fresh fruit can be used as garnish.

Serves 8

*See Glossary

The Chocolate Sauce

1 c. water
½ c. sugar
1 lb. chocolate

Bring water and sugar to a boil and slowly add the chocolate cut in small pieces. When melted, pour over cream puffs.

128

Judy's B & B

2036 Madrona Avenue • St. Helena, California 94574
(707) 963-3081

Surrounded by lush vineyards on the outskirts of picturesque St. Helena, Judy's B & B provides guests with a welcoming bottle of wine, warm personalized service and, most importantly, privacy. One large sitting-room-bedroom combination has a private bath and entrance, and is decorated to make guests feel relaxed and at home. Breakfast is served in your room each morning, or take your coffee on the sun-warmed pool deck. Bob and Judy Sculatti, innkeepers, will gladly arrange a myriad of activities from tours of the Hurd Candle Factory and local wineries, to renewing visits at the mineral baths, or glider and balloon flights, plus reservations at any of the superb local restaurants.

129

Brunch Bubble Ring

6 to 7 c. flour
1 c. sugar
1 T. salt
2 packages active dry yeast
1 c. milk
½ c. water
¾ c. butter or margarine
3 eggs
1½ c. raisins
¾ c. firmly packed brown sugar
1 T. cinnamon
1 c. chopped nuts
⅓ c. corn syrup for glazing

In large mixer bowl, combine 2 c. flour with sugar, salt and yeast. In small saucepan, heat milk, water and ½ c. butter until warm and butter is melted. Slowly add mixture to dry ingredients and using an electric mixer, beat 2 minutes at medium speed. Add eggs and 1½ c. more flour, beat at high speed 2 minutes, scraping sides of bowl. Stir in enough remaining flour to make a soft dough. Turn out onto floured board and knead until dough is smooth and satiny, adding flour as needed to prevent sticking. Knead in raisins. Cover with plastic wrap, then a towel. Let rest 20 minutes. Meanwhile, combine brown sugar, cinnamon and nuts in a small bowl. In small saucepan, melt remaining ¼ c. butter. Grease a 10" tube pan. Pinch off dough into 32 balls about 1" in diameter. Place 1 layer (16 balls) in tube pan. Brush with half of the melted butter and sprinkle with half of the brown sugar mixture. Place second layer of balls in pan and top with second half of melted butter and brown sugar mixture. Cover with plastic wrap and let dough stand at room temperature for 15 minutes. Dough will not appear doubled in size at this point. Bake at 375 degrees about

Brunch Bubble Ring (con't)

1 hour, until bread is nicely browned and sounds hollow when lightly tapped. If bread becomes overly brown while baking, cover with foil. Glaze surface with corn syrup, then let bread stand 10 minutes before removing from pan. Turn out onto wire rack and serve warm, pulling bread apart or slice when cool. Makes 1 10" round loaf.

Serves 8

Apple Cinnamon Muffins

1¾ c. flour
¾ t. salt
3 t. baking powder
½ t. cinnamon
1 egg, beaten
⅓ c. vegetable oil
¾ c. milk
1 c. apple, chopped

Topping Mix:

¼ t. cinnamon
2 T. sugar

In a large bowl, mix together dry ingredients. In medium-sized bowl, beat egg, add oil, milk and chopped apple. Add apple mixture to dry mixture. Mix only until moistened. Fill greased muffin cups ¾ full. Sprinkle with cinnamon sugar mixture. Bake at 400 degrees for about 15 minutes, or until golden.

Serves 4

Sour Cream Banana Bread

1 c. sugar
½ c. oil
2 eggs
1 c. mashed ripe banana
½ c. sour cream
1 t. vanilla
1½ c. flour
1 t. baking soda
½ t. salt

Heat oven to 350 degrees. Grease and flour bottom of 9" x 5" loaf pan. In large bowl, beat together sugar and oil. Add eggs, bananas, sour cream and vanilla; mix well. Lightly spoon flour into measuring cup, level off. Add flour, baking soda and salt, stir just until dry ingredients are moistened. Pour into prepared pan. Bake at 350 degrees for 50-60 minutes. Remove from pan. Cool completely. Wrap tightly and store in refrigerator. Makes 1 loaf.

Serves 6

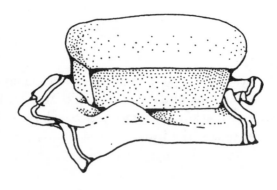

Ever Fresh Bran Muffins

3 c. whole bran cereal
2 c. buttermilk
1 c. water
½ c. cooking oil
2 eggs, beaten
1 c. packed brown sugar
1½ c. flour
2 t. baking powder
1 t. baking soda
1 t. salt
1½ c. raisins

Place bran cereal in large mixing bowl. Pour in buttermilk, water and oil; stir well. Mix in eggs and brown sugar. Add dry ingredients all at once. Stir just enough to combine. Fold in raisins. Store batter in tightly-covered container in refrigerator up to 6 weeks. To bake muffins, fill greased or paper lined muffin tins ⅔ full. Bake at 375 degrees for 20-25 minutes.

Yield: 30 muffins

133

THE FARMHOUSE
Country Bed and Breakfast

300 Taplin Road • St. Helena, California 94574
(707) 944-8430

You will feel like "invited guests" at The Farm House, a private residence that has opened its doors to discriminating travelers. There are three rooms at the Inn, a large one with private bath and two others in a separate wing that opens onto a veranda. There is a shared bath between them. On the lovely grounds a wisteria draped courtyard and lush vineyards which extend in every direction lend an air of relaxed romance. In the fall enjoy a Continental style breakfast in front of a friendly blaze in the "keeping room" or curl up with a good book and a cup of mulled wine in the cozy living room which also has a fireplace. For summer visitors, bring a swim-suit for a refreshing dip in the pool.

135

Carrot Muffins

2½ c. all-purpose flour
2 t. cinnamon
1 t. baking soda
1 t. baking powder
¾ t. nutmeg
½ t. salt
1½ c. white sugar
1 c. vegetable oil
3 large eggs
3 c. carrots, grated
1 c. walnuts, chopped

Preheat oven to 350 degrees. Combine flour, cinnamon, baking soda, baking powder, nutmeg and salt in a mixing bowl. Set aside. In another bowl, beat together the sugar, oil and eggs. Stir in grated carrots. Add dry ingredients and stir just to combine. Add nuts. Spoon batter into greased muffin cups ¾ full. Bake for 25 minutes. Cool and serve.

Serves 16

(For The Farmhouse by Mary Kerr)

136

Cinnamon Twists

1 package yeast
¼ c. warm water
1 c. buttermilk
6 T. butter
3 T. white sugar
1 t. salt
1 egg, slightly beaten
¼ t. soda
4 c. all-purpose white flour

Cinnamon Filling:

⅓ c. packed brown sugar, mixed with
½ t. cinnamon

Sprinkle yeast into warm water in a small bowl and stir to soften. Bring the buttermilk to a boil. Put 4 T. of the butter, sugar and salt in a large bowl. Pour in hot buttermilk and stir to melt butter. Let cool to lukewarm. Blend in the softened yeast, egg and soda. Gradually stir in the flour. Turn onto a floured board and knead until smooth and elastic. Invert bowl over dough and let stand 20 minutes. Punch dough down. Roll out to a 12" x 20" rectangle. Melt remaining 2 T. butter. Brush over surface. Sprinkle cinnamon filling lengthwise over half of dough. Fold in half to cover filling. Cut into strips. Twist and place on greased baking sheets. Let rise, uncovered, in a warm place about 45 minutes. Bake 10-12 minutes in a 375 degree oven. Remove; cool slightly before serving.

Serves 12

(For The Farmhouse by Mary Kerr)

137

Charles Krug

NAPA VALLEY
CABERNET SAUVIGNON

PRODUCED AND BOTTLED BY
CHARLES KRUG WINERY
ST. HELENA, CA, · BW 3110
ALCOHOL 13.0% BY VOLUME

The aroma is subtle and restrained, but shows rich Cabernet fruit.
Displays deep red-purplish color, with not a trace of amber
or age. The Charles Krug Vintage Select is ready for enjoyment
now but will mature significantly with five or more
years cellaring.

900 Meadowood Lane • St. Helena, California
(707) 963-3646
Hours: 6:00-9:00 p.m. Dinner, seven days a week
Credit Cards: Am. Express, Visa, M/C
Reservations: Suggested
Specialties: California Country Cuisine

The Meadowood in St. Helena is a secluded "private reserve" centered on 256 acres of terraced acres and groomed expanses of emerald lawns. The beautiful resort was once the local gentry's private playground and is now open to the public for executive retreats and romantic encounters. The main lodge has eleven rooms and suites surrounded by a challenging nine-hole golf course, championship tennis courts, Parcourse, a huge swimming pool and the Executive Conference Center. Throughout the expansive grounds are separate lodgings called cluster suites (four suites with an attached common room) to use for meetings or family get-togethers, and single units for privacy. Housed in the Executive Center is a banquet room, bar and lounge, meeting rooms and a restaurant made for romance where soft, subtle shades of fawn and white create a mood of intimate luxury. Chef Hale Lake treats diners to an awesome array of gourmet delights from the bounty of this rich valley. Near the pool is the aptly named Poolwatch Cafe which features delightful alfresco dining, and the Fairway Bar & Grill serves hearty breakfasts, luncheons and libations. Truly a one-of-a-kind luxury resort with everything for the discriminating guest.

139

Apple-Sweet Potato Vichyssoise

1½ c. sweet potatoes
½ stick butter
¼ c. shallots, chopped
¼ c. dry Vermouth
½ c. Granny Smith apples, peeled and diced
½ c. Golden Delicious apples, peeled
1 c. beef stock
1 c. chicken stock
1 c. cream
chives
salt and white pepper

Bake sweet potatoes in foil in a 350 degree F. oven until soft, about 1 hour. Cool.

Heat the butter in a saute pan. Add the shallots, vermouth and apples, and saute on moderate heat until soft, 5 minutes.

Put this mixture into the bowl of a processor along with the sweet potato pulp. Puree until smooth.

Push through a sieve and put into a saucepan along with the stock. Bring to a boil, reduce heat and simmer, covered, for 20 minutes on low heat. Add cream, chives, salt and pepper and serve.

Serves 6

Brandy Snap Cups

½ c. butter
½ c. sugar
⅓ c. molasses (use dark molasses for darker cup)
¼ t. ground ginger
1 t. orange rind, grated
¼ c. flour
2 T. cognac

Preheat oven to 300 degrees F. Have ready 3 glass ramekins or custard cups measuring about 4½" wide and 2" deep.

Combine the butter, sugar, molasses, ginger, cinnamon and orange rind in a saucepan and bring to a boil.

Remove from heat and stir in the flour, using a wire whisk. Add the cognac and stir. Blend until smooth. Set the saucepan in a basin of simmering water to prevent hardening as you work.

Drop the mixture a full tablespoon at a time onto an ungreased baking sheet. Space the tablespoons at wide intervals, remembering that they spread considerably as they bake. Prepare only 3 snaps at a time because the snaps harden fast once they are removed from the oven and they are difficult to shape.

Put the snaps in the oven and bake 14 minutes. When the snaps are removed from the oven, let them cool for a second or so. Run a thin spatula all around the perimeter of 1 snap at a time to loosen the bottom completely. Quickly place the snap inside 1 of the ramekins and press down to mold cup shapes. Let cool. If the snaps become impossible to scrape off, return the baking sheet briefly to the oven.

Continue preparing and baking the snaps until all the mixture

Brandy Snap Cups (con't)

is used.

To store: Arrange cups in a plastic or steel container and cover airtight in dark, cool, dry place. These can be made a day in advance if they are stored correctly.

Note: Darker snaps look better with light ice creams and lighter cups look best with dark ice creams.

Serves 8

To serve: Place brandy snap cups on dessert plates and fill with ice cream.

Lemon Curd

1 c. sugar

6 egg yolks, slightly beaten and strained (this prevents
any lumps)

½ c. lemon juice

¼ lb. butter (1 stick), unsalted, cut into small pieces

1 T. lemon peel, grated

Combine the sugar and egg yolks in a medium-sized saucepan;
stir in the lemon juice gradually. Cook over low heat, stirring constantly until the mixture coats the back of a spoon and registers
168 degrees on a candy thermometer. *Do not boil.* Remove from
heat; whisk until slightly cool. Stir in butter and grated lemon
peel. Cool completely.

Serves 12

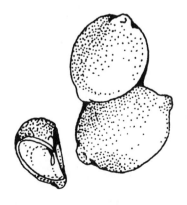

Villa St. Helena

2727 Sulphur Springs Avenue • St. Helena, California 94574
(707) 963-2514

The 12,000 square foot Villa St. Helena is ensconced on a twenty-acre estate of manicured lawns and well-trimmed vineyards with panoramic views of the Napa Valley and the pastoral village of St. Helena. The three-story Mediterranean-style villa, designed by internationally renowned architect Robert Carerre, was built into a rounding hillside to maximize distant romantic vistas. A combination of muted earth tones, brick and tile effortlessly balances country comfort with easy elegance. All the rooms have private entrances from verandas that lead to a quiet courtyard with a swimming pool. Sip complimentary fine wines in the library and enjoy a Continental breakfast in the sun-drenched solarium.

Prune Bread

1 12-oz. package moist-pack pitted prunes
½ c. port wine
1½ c. whole wheat flour, unsifted
½ c. all-purpose flour, unsifted
1 t. salt
1 t. soda
½ t. baking powder
½ t. cinnamon
¼ c. butter
¾ c. brown sugar, packed
1 egg
1 c. buttermilk
1 T. port wine
⅔ c. chopped walnuts

Chop the prunes and place in bowl with port wine. Allow to soak for 15 minutes.

Stir together the whole wheat and all-purpose flour, salt, soda, baking powder and cinnamon until thoroughly mixed. Set aside. In a separate bowl, beat together the butter and brown sugar until creamy, then beat in the egg. Alternately add flour mixture and buttermilk plus 1 T. of port wine to the creamed mixture. With the last addition of flour, add prunes and nuts, stirring until well blended. Pour into a well-greased 9" x 5" loaf pan.

Bake at 350 degrees for about 1 hour and 10 minutes or until bread begins to pull away from sides of pan and when tested with wood toothpick or skewer in center comes out clean. Let cool in pan ten minutes; then turn out onto a wire rack to cool.

Makes 1 loaf

Villa Apple Cake

3 c. flour
1 t. soda
1 t. salt
1½ c. oil
3 eggs
2 c. sugar
2 t. vanilla
1 c. pecans, chopped
3 c. apples, chopped

Glaze:

½ c. butter
1 c. brown sugar
¼ c. milk

Sift together dry ingredients and in a separate bowl mix oil, eggs, sugar and vanilla. Combine wet and dry ingredients. Fold in nuts and apples. Pour into an oiled bundt pan or tube pan. Bake at 350 degrees for 1 hour 15 minutes.

To make glaze, melt butter in sauce pan, add brown sugar and milk and cook for 3 minutes. Pour over hot cake. Let stand for 2 hours, then unmold and serve.

Makes 1 cake

148

Larkmead Country Inn

1103 Larkmead Lane • Calistoga, California 94515
(707) 942-5360

Screened by striking sycamore, cypress and magnolia trees, the Larkmead Country Inn presents a quiet respite from the accelerated pace of today's life. Situated on Larkmead Lane, and converted from a family home by Gene and Joan Garbarino, the Italianate-style Inn reflects a subtly elegant atmosphere with Persian carpets, European antiques, and fine old paintings and prints. The sprawling white clapboard house features four large bedrooms, with private baths, named for the fine wines produced in the Napa Valley. You'll love the added personal touches of fresh cut flowers and a decanter of wine in each room. A Continental breakfast is served in the formal dining room or during the spring and summer on the expansive porches.

149

Scones Larkmead

1¾ c. sifted all-purpose flour
2¼ t. double acting baking powder
1 T. sugar
½ t. salt
¼ c. butter, cut into bits
2 eggs
⅓ c. cream

Sift all dry ingredients together into a large bowl. Cut butter into flour mixture until it resembles a coarse meal. In a separate bowl beat eggs, reserve 2 T. for brushing the tops of the scones. Beat cream into eggs and add this to the flour. Quickly combine and place dough on a floured surface. Pat until ¾" thick and round. Cut with a knife into diamond-shaped wedges. Brush with reserved egg and sprinkle with sugar. Bake in a preheated 450 degree oven for 15 minutes.

Yield: 6-8 scones

Pumpkin Muffins Larkmead

1⅓ c. all-purpose flour
½ c. sugar
2 t. double-acting baking powder
½ t. salt
½ t. cinnamon
½ t. freshly grated nutmeg (or preground nutmeg)
½ stick (¼ c.) cold unsalted butter cut into bits
½ c. raisins
½ c. canned pumpkin puree
½ c. milk
1 large egg, lightly beaten

Butter and flour a 12-muffin tin and set aside. Sift into a large bowl all dry ingredients. Blend flour mixture with butter until it resembles coarse meal. Add remaining ingredients and stir until just combined. Place batter in muffin tin and bake in preheated oven of 400 degrees for 18-20 minutes. Let muffins cool in tin on a rack for 10 minutes more and then invert onto the rack.

Yield: 1 dozen muffins

Guenoc

Lake County
Cabernet Sauvignon

Produced and Bottled by Guenoc Winery
Middletown, California Alcohol 13.0% by Volume

A full-bodied wine; elegant, complex, rich and luscious
with distinct varietal character.

A fine accompaniment to meat entrees.

CALISTOGA INN

1250 Lincoln Avenue • Calistoga, California 94515
(707) 942-4101

Relax and renew yourself in the serenity of picturesque Calistoga at The Calistoga Inn, a landmark building constructed at the turn of the century and renovated in the late 1970's by Phillip Rogers. Although there are seventeen rooms in the Inn, the undeniable star is its restaurant, which specializes in seafood from the Pacific North Coast, and has been acclaimed by leading food critics as one of California's finest. The experience of the kitchen staff is mirrored in the tested yet simple methods of grilling, sauteing, poaching, uncomplicated sauces, and fresh herb and nut butters. To accompany that special dish the wine list affords an extensive choice, including some vintages rarely found outside the Napa Valley.

153

Red Bell Pepper and Tomato Soup

½ lb. yellow onions
2 leeks
⅛ lb. sweet butter
4 T. olive oil
1 lb. red bell peppers, seeded and deveined
1 qt. chicken stock
½ lb. tomatoes, seeded
1 c. cream
dash each of cayenne, white pepper and salt

Chop onions and white part of leeks and slowly saute in butter and olive oil until limp (do not brown). Add bell pepper and "sweat" on low flame for 10 minutes. Add chicken stock and bring to a boil. Add tomatoes, reduce heat and simmer 20 minutes. In a blender or food processor fitted with the steel knife blade, puree the mixture and strain. Add the cream but do not let the soup boil again. Season with cayenne, salt and pepper.

Serves 6

Calistoga Inn Crab Cakes with Avocado Butter

1 c. milk
1 bay leaf
1 T. sweet butter
¼ c. celery, finely chopped
¼ c. onion, finely chopped
¼ c. bell pepper, finely chopped
1 T. parsley
1 T. seasoned flour
¼ t. salt
1 t. white pepper
1 lb. crab meat, carefully picked over
1 c. seasoned flour
2 eggs, lightly beaten
½ c. cornmeal mixed with
½ c. bread crumbs

Scald the milk in a stainless steel pan with the bay leaf and set aside. Melt the butter in a separate saucepan, add the vegetables and parsley and cook until the onion appears transparent. Add flour, stirring the entire time with wooden spoon. Remove the bay leaf and pour the hot milk into the flour and vegetable mixture. Return to the stove and cook for 5 minutes stirring continuously. Add the salt and pepper. Squeeze the excess water from the crab meat and add to the mixture, remove from the stove and cool. Once cooled, measure into 1½-oz. portions, roll and flatten into cakes. Dip first into the seasoned flour and then into the egg, then into the bread crumb-cornmeal mixture. Refrigerate at least 1 hour. Deep fry at 350 degrees until brown. The crab cakes may be reheated in the oven. Serve with Avocado Butter (recipe follows).

Serves 5

Avocado Butter

1½ T. shallots, chopped
½ c. white wine
salt and pepper to taste
¼ c. fresh lemon juice
lemon zest
1 ripe avocado
½ lb. butter

Combine shallots and wine in a stainless sauce pan. Place over heat and reduce by half, let cool and add salt, pepper, lemon juice and lemon zest. In a food processor, cream the avocado and the butter until smooth. Add in the reduced wine mixture slowly until fully incorporated.

Smoked Salmon Mousse with Black Caviar

⅛ lb. smoked salmon
½ c. cream cheese
½ t. lemon zest
1 t. lemon juice
1 T. grated red onion
3 T. black lumpfish caviar, rinsed and drained if too salty

Puree salmon in food processor. Add cream cheese, lemon zest and juice, red onion and puree until smooth. Place in pastry bag fitted with the large star tip. Pipe into decorative mounds and spoon caviar over the top. Serve with large croutons or crackers. Garnish with lemon slices, lettuce and parsley as desired.

Serves 6

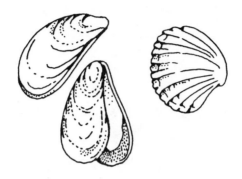

Fish Stew Calistoga Inn

1 c. celery, chopped
1 c. onion, chopped
1 c. carrots, chopped
¼ c. white part of leek, chopped
2 T. olive oil
1 c. pear tomatoes, chopped and seeded
1 qt. fish stock
2 T. garlic, minced
pinch of saffron
2 T. fennel seed
2 c. dry vermouth
cayenne pepper, white pepper and salt to taste
2 lbs. assorted fish and shellfish (swordfish, rockcod,
    salmon, clams, scallops, mussels, etc.)

Saute onion, celery, carrots and leeks in olive oil. Add tomatoes,
fish stock and let simmer. In another pan saute the garlic and
when clear, add saffron and the fennel seed. Add the vermouth
and reduce to a glaze. Add this to the stock. Season with cayenne
pepper, white pepper and salt. Using the assorted fish and shellfish
cook in stock over low heat until fish is done.

Serves 4-6

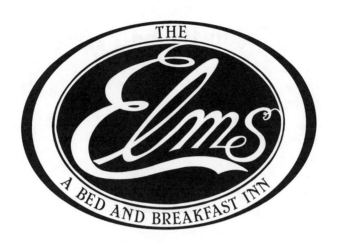

THE

Elms

A BED AND BREAKFAST INN

1300 Cedar Street • Calistoga, California 94515
(707) 942-9476

Marc and Diane Harris have turned one of the "Eight Great" homes of Calistoga (it's listed in the National Register of Historic Places) into a new and most gracious Bed and Breakfast Inn. The Elms bespeaks a quiet Victorian elegance that transports guests back in time and the tasteful rooms reflect the ambiance of the period. A full gourmet breakfast is served, and Marc and Diane host a wine and cheese hour each afternoon. They will also gladly arrange various activities as well as appointments at the mud baths.

159

Cajun Baked Eggs

6 eggs
½ c. water
1 c. whipping cream
1 t. salt
2 t. stone ground mustard
½ t. pepper
1 t. tabasco sauce
¼ c. butter
5 green onions, chopped
1½ c. mushrooms, coarsely chopped
1 small green bell pepper, chopped
3 medium garlic cloves, minced
1 c. cheddar cheese, shredded
2 t. paprika

Preheat oven to 300 degrees. Combine eggs, water, whipping cream, salt, stone ground mustard, pepper and tabasco sauce. Whisk until eggs are frothy; set aside. In 12" skillet melt butter and saute vegetables until onions are transparent. Whisk egg mixture again and add to vegetables in skillet; blend well. Sprinkle with cheddar cheese and paprika. Bake in skillet for about 30-35 minutes or until set. Remove from oven and let stand for about 5 minutes. Cut into pie wedges and serve.

Serves 8

Raspberry-Apple Crumble

7 firm apples, McIntosh, Red or Golden Delicious
1 package (12 oz.) frozen raspberries, thawed, drained
   (reserve juice)
8 T. sugar

Crumble Topping:

1 c. flour
6 T. butter, softened
½ c. sugar

Cut flour, butter and sugar together until mixture is crumbly.

Preheat oven to 350 degrees. Butter 8 4" round ramekins. Peel, core and slice apples. In each ramekin place a layer of sliced apples, then about 2 T. of raspberries; sprinkle 1 t. of sugar on top of berries, then top with another layer of apples and 2 T. of the reserved juice. Sprinkle generous amount of crumble topping on top.
Bake for 20-30 minutes.

Serves 8

Marinated Grapefruit

3 grapefruits, halved
¼ c. butter, melted
¼ cup Grand Marnier
2 t. sugar

Cut around every section of grapefruit, close to membrane (fruit should be completely loosened from shell). Combine melted butter, Grand Marnier and sugar. Drizzle over cut fruit. Let stand at room temperature about 2 hours to marinate. Broil in shallow baking dish 4" from heat about 10 minutes, or long enough to brown tops and until bubbling hot.

Serves 6

Pain Perdu or Lost Bread

⅓ c. vegetable oil
6 eggs
3 T. Grand Marnier or triple sec
2 T. milk
⅓ c. sugar
grated zest from 1 large lemon
12 slices French bread or raisin bread
powdered sugar
butter
syrup

In heavy skillet over medium heat, heat oil. In medium bowl, combine eggs, liqueur, milk, sugar and lemon zest. Whisk until eggs are frothy and sugar is dissolved. When oil is hot, dip bread slices into egg mixture, turning to coat well. Place bread in hot oil in batches. Fry until golden brown on both sides, turning once. Drain on paper towels; sprinkle with powdered sugar. Keep warm in oven while frying the remaining slices. Serve hot with butter and syrup.

Serves 6

Winter Snow-Capped Peaches

1 can (29 oz.) peach halves (reserve nectar)
butter
brown sugar
peach brandy
miniature marshmallows

Preheat oven to 250 degrees. Arrange peach slices cut side up in shallow baking dish. In each peach half place a small lump of butter, 1 t. brown sugar, ½ t. peach brandy, and 3 miniature marshmallows. Pour ½ c. of the peach nectar in bottom of dish and heat for 15-20 minutes or until marshmallows are puffed.

Serves 4

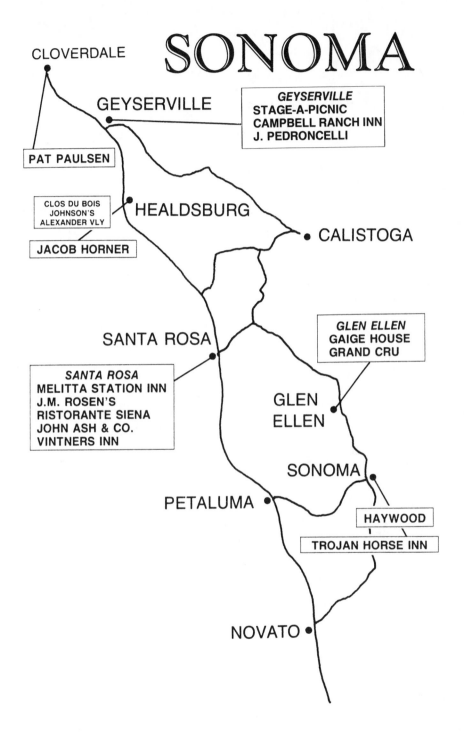

SONOMA

CLOVERDALE

GEYSERVILLE

GEYSERVILLE
STAGE-A-PICNIC
CAMPBELL RANCH INN
J. PEDRONCELLI

PAT PAULSEN

HEALDSBURG

CLOS DU BOIS
JOHNSON'S
ALEXANDER VLY

JACOB HORNER

CALISTOGA

SANTA ROSA

SANTA ROSA
MELITTA STATION INN
J.M. ROSEN'S
RISTORANTE SIENA
JOHN ASH & CO.
VINTNERS INN

GLEN ELLEN
GAIGE HOUSE
GRAND CRU

GLEN
ELLEN

SONOMA

PETALUMA

HAYWOOD

TROJAN HORSE INN

NOVATO

163

TROJAN HORSE INN

19455 Sonoma Highway • Sonoma, California 95476
(707) 996-2430

The North Coast is delightful in any season, and what better way to enjoy the area than with a stay at the Trojan Horse Inn? Located among the historic and the new of downtown Sonoma, the Inn offers comfort and convenience. Built in the late 1880's and restored by Ms. Fields and Mr. Anton, the mansion is filled with charming antiques from the late 1880's and early 1890's. There are eight lovely rooms at the spacious Inn, some with private baths, and each is furnished to appeal to the most discriminating guest. At the heart of the Inn is the King's Room for cozy evenings sipping wine in front of a cheery fireplace. The Sonoma Creek runs through the rear of the garden and provides a musical backdrop to the patio and BBQ area. Every morning a hearty breakfast is served from 8:00 a.m. to 9:30 a.m. in the dining room.

165

Herbed Baked Eggs

1 t. melted butter or non-stick vegetable spray
2 eggs
1 t. cream
3 T. cheese (cheddar or Sonoma Jack), grated
chervil or dill

Butter or spray individual ramekins and break the eggs into them. Add the cream and cover with cheese. Sprinkle chervil or dill over top and bake for 12-15 minutes in preheated oven set at 400 degrees.

Serves 1

Saucy Sausage Waffles

1 c. waffle mix
½ c. milk
3 oz. applesauce
⅛ c. oil
1 egg
3 oz. pork sausage, cooked and crumbled

To prepare waffles, mix all ingredients together in large bowl. Make sure mixture is well combined. Cook in waffle iron and serve with Spiced Apple Syrup (recipe follows).

Serves 4

Spiced Apple Syrup

2 c. apples, peeled and sliced
6 oz. can frozen apple juice concentrate
4 cans water
¼ t. allspice
½ c. sugar

To prepare syrup bring all ingredients to a boil and cook until apples are soft. Thicken (if necessary) with cornstarch. Divide syrup into four equal parts and use one for waffles. Refrigerate the rest.

13540 Arnold Drive • Glen Ellen, California 95442
(707) 935-0237

Nestled in the Valley of the Moon, surrounded by gentle green hills, you'll find the stately Gaige House where historical and natural charm abound in the lovely valley Jack London called home. Styled in an Italianate Queen Anne motif, the Inn was originally built in the 1890's and renovated in 1980. The cozy rooms are uniquely furnished with collected antiques and include all the modern conveniences while retaining the quiet ambiance of another time. One of the recent additions to the Inn is a spacious deck built around ancient oaks and overhanging the musical Calabezas Creek. Each morning awake refreshed and treat yourself to a hearty breakfast in the dining room or on the sunny deck. After a busy day of touring wineries and sightseeing relax before dinner in the parlor over complimentary hors d'oeuvres and wine while your hosts make dinner reservations at any of the wonderful, nearby restaurants.

Apple-Raisin-Walnut Crepes with Creme Fraiche

Sauce:

6 T. sour cream
1½ c. heavy cream
4-5 T. (or more) real maple syrup

Crepes:

2 eggs
1 c. milk
1 c. flour
¼ c. melted butter

Filling:

4 large Granny Smith apples, cored, peeled and thickly sliced
¼ c. butter
¼-⅓ c. molasses, light or dark
½ c. raisins
½ c. walnuts, coarsely chopped

To prepare the sauce, stir the sour cream, then gradually add the heavy cream. Allow to stand at room temperature for approximately 1-2 hours. (The mixture will thicken as it stands.) Sweeten to taste with the maple syrup. If it becomes too thick add a little

Apple-Raisin-Walnut Crepes (con't)

more cream and check sweetening. Refrigerate to retard thickening too much and begin the crepes.

Place all ingredients for the crepes in the bowl of a food processor or blender and combine thoroughly. Cook the crepes over medium heat in a lightly oiled crepe or frying pan, using a scant ¼ c. for each one. (Makes 1 dozen 6" crepes.) Keep them warm and prepare the filling.

Simmer the apples in the butter until they begin to soften, gently turning to cook evenly. Add the molasses, continue to simmer until the crispness of the apples is gone, but not mushy. Fold in the raisins and walnuts, and heat thoroughly.

To assemble the crepes place a large spoonful of hot fruit onto the crepe and fold it. Place 2 folded crepes on a serving plate and ladle ¼-⅓ c. of the sauce over the top.

Serves 6

Sausage and Cheese Quiche

¾ lb. fresh pork sausage
½ small onion, chopped
1½ t. dried sage
1 9-inch pie crust, partially baked
1 c. Sonoma Jack cheese, grated
1 c. cheddar (medium cheddar works well), grated
3 eggs
2 c. half-and-half

Crumble and fry the sausage with the onion and sage, cooking well but browning only slightly. Cool. Prebake the pastry shell by lining it with aluminum foil and filling it with pinto beans or other beans for weight. Place it in a 450 degree oven for 6-7 minutes. Remove the shell from the oven and take off the foil and beans, return to oven and bake for another 4 minutes or un-

171

Sausage and Cheese Quiche (con't)

til it begins to brown. Cool slightly. Spread the sausage mixture evenly into the pie shell and sprinkle the cheeses over the meat. Pour the eggs, which have been beaten together with the half-and-half, carefully over the cheese. Bake 45-50 minutes at 375 degrees or until the quiche has set and the top is golden brown.

Serves 6

Banana-Walnut Sourdough Wheatcakes

1¾ c. whole wheat flour
½ c. sourdough starter (recipe follows)
2 c. buttermilk, warmed
2 eggs
¼ c. evaporated milk
¼ c. melted butter
1-3 T. sugar (depending on buttermilk and starter)
1 t. baking soda
½ t. salt
2 large, very ripe bananas
½-⅔ c. walnuts, chopped

Beat together flour, starter and buttermilk. Cover and let stand at room temperature for 45-60 minutes, or in refrigerator overnight. Beat eggs, milk and butter into flour mixture, then stir in the sugar, soda and salt. Mash the bananas well, add walnuts and the banana to the batter, stir until well blended. Heat a griddle to moderately hot, butter it lightly and cook the pancakes to desired degree of doneness. Serve with plenty of butter and real maple syrup.

Serves 6-8

172

Sourdough Starter

1 T. dry yeast
¼ c. 110 degree water
1 c. milk
1 c. all purpose flour
1 t. sugar

Dissolve the yeast in the water in a large ceramic bowl. Stir in the milk, flour and sugar. Cover and let stand at room temperature for 2 or 3 days. Stir down if necessary during the first few hours. Store covered, in the refrigerator. Replenish as used with equal portions of flour and milk.

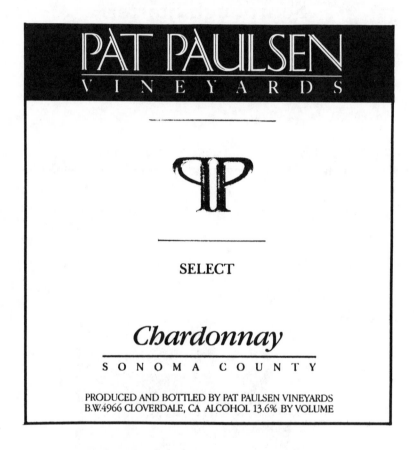

SELECT

Chardonnay

S O N O M A   C O U N T Y

PRODUCED AND BOTTLED BY PAT PAULSEN VINEYARDS
B.W.4966 CLOVERDALE, CA ALCOHOL 13.6% BY VOLUME

Elements of honeyed apricots, cinnamon, cloves and sweet ripe apples generously flesh out the tight, medium-bodied structure of this wine.

Enjoy this wine with seafood, veal and chicken.

174

5850 Melita Road • Santa Rosa, California 95405
(707) 538-7712

In the heart of wine country, in the Valley of the Moon, sits the rustic Melitta Station Inn. The historic structure was a stagecoach stop that has been converted into a charming six room Inn and family home by Diane and Jeff Jefferds. Each room has its own private bath and is comfortably furnished with antiques, country collectables and hand-stenciled furniture. The feeling of peaceful country living is enhanced by surrounding wineries, quaint villages, rolling hills and smooth green meadows. Savor the fragrance of the pepperwood trees and the innkeepers' herb garden while enjoying a Continental breakfast of various baked breads, fruits and steaming cups of fresh ground coffee on the balcony. In the evening sip complimentary wine and relax in the cozy sitting room.

Yogurt and Green Chili Corn Bread

½ c. flour
2 t. baking powder
1 t. baking soda
⅓ t. salt
1½ c. yellow corn meal
⅓ c. dark brown sugar
1 extra large egg
1 c. plain yogurt
¼ c. canned green chilies, diced
¼ c. sharp cheddar cheese, grated

Mix all dry ingredients in a large bowl and make a well in the center. Beat the egg with the yogurt and pour into the well. Mix a few strokes and add chilies and cheese. Spread into 8" cast iron skillet. Bake at 350 degrees for 30-35 minutes, or until center springs back when touched. Cool at least 10 minutes and invert onto serving plate. To serve, slice into pie-shaped wedges.

Serves 6-8

Raisin Soda Bread With Orange Peel and Caraway Seeds

8 c. flour
1½ t. salt
6 t. baking powder
2 t. baking soda
1 c. currants or raisins
4 t. caraway seeds
peel of 1 orange

Raisin Soda Bread (con't)

1 c. sugar
½ c. butter
2 extra-large eggs
3 c. buttermilk

Mix first 8 ingredients together and cut in butter until crumbly. Beat eggs and buttermilk together and combine with dry ingredients. Knead 2 minutes and divide dough into 4 equal parts. Freeze each one. To bake take ¼ portion of dough and place in a well greased 6" cast iron skillet. Cut a large cross in the top and bake at 400 degrees for 20 minutes.

Serves 4-6

Mint or Basil Frittata

4 medium potatoes
4 t. safflower oil
4 T. fresh mint or basil, chopped
1 t. salt
pepper to taste
8 eggs, lightly beaten
2 T. butter

Boil the potatoes until tender, then peel and dice. Heat oil in a cast iron skillet and saute potatoes over moderate heat, about 5 minutes or until they begin to brown. Preheat oven to 475 degrees. Combine mint or basil, salt and pepper with the beaten eggs. Add butter to skillet containing potatoes. When it's hot add egg mixture. Stir slightly until it begins to set. Then put in oven on highest rack for 15-20 minutes and the top begins to brown.

Serves 6

Apple Oatmeal Muffins

2 c. oatmeal
2 c. flour
½ t. salt
1 t. baking soda
3 t. baking powder
1 c. brown sugar
1 c. oil
2 eggs, beaten
2 c. buttermilk
1 c. apples, chopped, unpeeled
cinnamon
sugar

Combine first 6 ingredients. Stir with fork and add oil, eggs, buttermilk and chopped apple. Stir and place mixture in a very small muffin tin. Bake at 350 degrees for 15 minutes. When the muffins are cool enough to handle dip the tops in the cinnamon and sugar. This batter also keeps very nicely in the refrigerator for up to 2 weeks.

Yield: many

135 4th Street • Santa Rosa, California 95401
(707) 544-9550
Hours: 5:00-11:00 p.m. Weeknights
5:00 p.m.-?? Weekends
Credit Cards: M/C, Visa
Prices: Moderate
Reservations: Suggested
Specialties: Eclectic

Crisp, clean modern lines combined with an intricately carved back bar from the 1880's, antiques and Murano glass chandeliers set the stage for fine dining at J.M. Rosen's Restaurant in Santa Rosa. An extensive wine list which includes some of the best from Napa and Sonoma plus some excellent imported vintages accents a menu of eclectic specialties. Consider tempting appetizers of Beluga Caviar and Smoked Salmon in Olive Oil and follow with a crisp Caesar or Spinach Salad. Next, sample intriguing entrees such as Veal T-Bone with Raspberry Mustard Sauce, Duck Cassis or Stuffed Quail with Apple Brandy Sauce, each guaranteed to tantalize the most discriminating palate. For a grand finale to the perfect meal, a delicately textured slice of Rosen's "world famous" cheesecake will send anyone home smiling in satisfaction.

179

Garlic Chicken

4 4-oz. chicken breasts, skinned
1 T. flour
pinch of parsley for color
1 oz. clarified butter*
1 oz. brandy
4 oz. white wine
2 whole tomatoes, cooked and peeled
4 cloves garlic, minced
3 large mushrooms, sliced
pinch of parsley for color
2 T. sweet butter

Dredge chicken breasts in flour. Saute chicken in clarified butter on both sides. Add brandy, white wine, tomatoes, garlic, mushrooms and parsley; simmer. Add butter to thicken sauce. Remove chicken; place on dish and pour sauce over.

Serves 2

*See Glossary

180

Veal Piccata

8 oz. veal loins, cut and pounded into 1 oz. paper thin slices
flour for dredging
1 oz. clarified butter*
1 c. white wine
2 T. capers
½ t. garlic
2 T. butter
juice of 1 whole lemon

Add clarified butter to a saute pan, heat. Dredge veal in flour and quickly saute. Remove veal to heated platter and deglaze* pan with white wine. Add remaining ingredients and reduce. Sauce will thicken on its own. Shake pan over flame. More butter may be added toward the end to thicken. Pour sauce over veal.

Serves 2

*See Glossary

Scampi

½ lb. prawns
clarified butter*
½ c. white wine
2 oz. cooking sherry
½ T. garlic, minced
1 T. shallots, finely chopped
pinch of parsley
2 T. butter

Saute prawns in clarified butter, turning carefully. Add white wine, sherry, garlic, shallots and parsley. Reduce heat and add butter. This sauce does *not* thicken. When prawns are pink, it's done. The larger the prawn, the better.

Variation: Boil up some angel pasta, and pour scampi over. *The best!*

Serves 2

*See Glossary

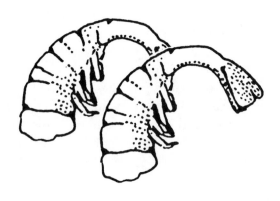

·RISTORANTE·
at Parkpoint

1229 North Dutton Avenue • Santa Rosa, California 95401
(707) 578-4511
Hours: 7:00-10:30 a.m., Breakfast, Mon.-Fri.
11:30 a.m.-2:30 p.m., Lunch, Mon.-Fri.
4:30 p.m., Cocktails, Wed.-Fri.
6:00-9:30 p.m., Dinner, Wed.-Sun.
10:00 a.m.-2:00 p.m., Sunday Brunch
Prices: Moderate
Credit Cards: M/C, Visa
Specialties: Innovative Italian Cuisine,
Homemade Pastas, and European Style Pizza

The Ristorante Siena affords the finest in Italian dining, be it in the inviting atmosphere of the Cafe, the informality of the sun-warmed terrace, the elegance of the formal dining room or just a quick antipasto after work at the beer and wine bar. Built by the Hirschberg brothers, Michael and Alex of Restaurant Matisse fame, the ristorante is located in an active business park. It "caters" to the neighbors with "Business Breakfasts," special reservations, and deliveries of signature pasta, European pizza, sandwiches and luncheon salads. For dinner, savor one of the innovative entrees with a glass of fine wine while listening to the soft strains of a guitar. The entrees include seven different homemade pastas (available in half orders as an appetizer), grilled seafood and chicken, plus premium veal with four different sauces. For something different on Sundays, relax and enjoy a Champagne Brunch with an Italian flair.

183

Ravioli with
Spinach Ricotta Filling

Filling:

3 bunches spinach, washed and picked over
¼ c. onion, finely chopped
¼ lb. butter
1 c. ricotta cheese
½ c. parmesan cheese
2 egg yolks
½ t. fresh black pepper
½ t. nutmeg

Dough:

2 eggs
1½ c. flour
2 T. milk

Blanch spinach in large pot of boiling water for 30 seconds or until just wilted. Drain and refresh with cold water. Finely chop spinach and press out remaining moisture. Saute onion in butter for 2 minutes, then add spinach and cook 1 or 2 minutes longer or until spinach is dry, and butter has been absorbed. Mix the remaining ingredients in a bowl and then fold in the spinach and taste for seasoning; add salt if necessary. Set aside.

Combine the ingredients for the dough. Vigorously work them together and then knead for several minutes. Cover and set aside until ready to use. *To assemble the raviolis:* roll out the dough as thinly as possible or use a pasta machine which will produce 6" wide strips. Hand rolled dough should be cut into similarly wide bands. Take a strip of pasta and paint it with water to insure filling will stick. Keep remaining strips covered until ready to use. Place little balls of filling (2-3 t. each) across a sheet of pasta, spacing

Ravioli with Spinach Ricotta Filling (con't)

them 1½-2" apart. Paint the top sheet of pasta with water and press the 2 wet sides together. Press down the dough with your fingers in all the spaces between the mounds of filling. Cut into individual squares with a ravioli wheel. To cook the raviolis, bring a large pot of water to a boil. Add salt and oil, and cook the raviolas for 6-7 minutes. Drain and top with your favorite sauce, or simply toss with melted butter, chopped fresh herbs and parmesan cheese.

Serves 6

Filet of Salmon Milanese

1 egg
2 T. cream
1 c. bread crumbs
1 c. freshly grated Parmesan cheese
½ t. pepper
1 t. basil
1 t. oregano
4 6-oz. salmon fillets
butter
olive oil
lemon wedges

Combine egg and cream in shallow bowl. In a second bowl combine the bread crumbs, cheese, pepper and herbs. Dip the fillets into the egg mixture and then the bread crumb mixture. Coat generously and let stand several minutes before proceeding. Heat equal parts of butter and olive oil in a skillet. Fry the fillets until just cooked through and golden brown on both sides. Serve garnished with lemon wedges.

Serves 4

Osso Buco, Milanese

1 c. carrot, finely chopped
1 c. onion, finely chopped
1 c. celery, finely chopped
2 cloves garlic, finely minced
2 bay leaves
2 T. parsley, chopped
Pinch each of lemon zest, thyme and black pepper
3 veal shanks, sawed into rounds, 1½" thick
flour for dredging
salt and pepper to taste
2 T. oil
1 c. white wine
2 plus c. veal stock (or 1 c. beef bouillion)
1½ c. tomato, chopped

Saute chopped carrot, onion and celery in butter until just soft, but do not brown. Add garlic, bay leaves, parsley, lemon zest, thyme and pepper. Place in bottom of baking pan or casserole. Tie veal shanks with string to secure and dredge in flour seasoned with salt and pepper. Brown the pieces in hot oil and spread them over vegetables. Deglaze* the pan with wine, scraping any browned bits adhering to the pan. Add the stock and tomato. Bring to a boil. Pour the boiling mixture over the meat so as to just cover the shanks. Add more stock and/or tomato juice if necessary. Cover casserole (top dish with foil) and cook in a preheated oven for about 2 hours at 350 degrees. Check the veal shanks once or twice to see they remain submerged in the sauce. When fully cooked the shanks will be very soft and tender. Remove the string and arrange them on a serving plate. Check sauce for seasonings and adjust accordingly. If sauce seems thick add a little stock. If

Osso Buco, Milanese (con't)

it seems too thin reduce it some by boiling down quickly. Serve
with Mock Risotto (recipe follows).

Serves 6

*See Glossary

Mock Risotto

4½ c. chicken stock
3 t. onion, minced
3 T. butter
2 c. white rice
salt and pepper
chopped parsley
2 T. proscuitto, chopped
½ c. Parmesan cheese, grated
juice of 1 lemon

Bring stock to a boil and reduce it to simmer. In a separate pan
saute onion in butter until soft. Add rice and saute briefly. Season
lightly with salt and pepper. Add the boiling stock. Bring rice
to a boil, then cover and reduce heat to low. Cook 15-20 minutes.
Let stand 5-10 minutes more. When ready to serve, stir in parsley,
proscuitto, Parmesan cheese and lemon juice with perhaps a pat
or two of soft butter. Serve extra Parmesan on the side.

Serves 6

187

Filet of Salmon
with Sorrel Sauce

3 T. butter
4 6-oz. salmon fillets
½ c. white wine
1 T. shallots, minced
½ c. fish stock (optional)
¼ c. heavy cream
¾ stick butter
½ c. sorrel, cut into strips

Heat the butter in a non-reactive skillet. Sear the fillets gently (don't brown) on both sides. Add the wine and shallots to the pan and cover with a lid or buttered wax paper. Finish cooking in 375 degree oven or on top of stove over *low* heat. Remove the fish when done and place on a warm serving plate. Add the fish stock or more wine and the cream to the pan. Reduce until thick and syrupy. Swirl small chunks of butter into the reduction. Warm gently if necessary but do not allow the butter to "break". Stir in the chopped sorrel and pour over the fish.

Serves 4

Chicken Toscana

6 breasts of chicken, boned
flour for dredging
4 T. butter, divided
½ lb. mushrooms, sliced
1½ c. tomatoes, peeled, seeded and chopped
2 dozen cured black olives
1 c. veal stock
1 c. tomato sauce
1 T. garlic, chopped
1 c. red wine
salt and pepper
chopped parsley for garnish

Dredge the chicken in the flour and saute slowly in a large skillet with 2 T. of the butter. Finish cooking (approximately 5 minutes) in oven or on top of stove, covered. When the chicken is done, remove from the skillet. Add the remaining butter and saute the mushrooms. Add tomato, olives, stock, tomato sauce, garlic and red wine. Cook until reduced and somewhat syrupy. Taste for seasoning and add salt and pepper if necessary. Return chicken to pan just to reheat. Arrange the pieces on a platter and top with the parsley.

Serves 6

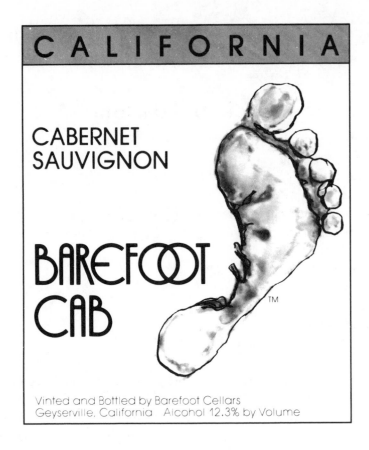

CALIFORNIA

CABERNET
SAUVIGNON

BAREFOOT
CAB ™

Vinted and Bottled by Barefoot Cellars
Geyserville, California   Alcohol 12.3% by Volume

Barefoot Cab is award winning Cabernet Sauvignon wine,
very affordable and accessible. Available in 1.5L Magnums.
Enough for cooking and enjoying with meals.
It has the blackberry and cherry aroma of young Cabernet,
with the aged complexity of oak. The soft and spicy finish
will appeal to new and experienced palates alike.

Perfect with red pastas, soups and sharp cheeses; stands up to
spicy foods and seasoned vegetables; ideal with all meats.

190

JOHN ASH & CO.

RESTAURANT AND WINE SHOP

4350 Barnes Road • Santa Rosa, California 95401
(707) 527-7687
Hours: 11:30 a.m.-2:30 p.m. Lunch, Mon.-Fri.
6:00-9:00 p.m. Dinner, Tues.-Sun.
10:30 a.m.-2:30 p.m. Sunday Brunch
Credit Cards: Visa, M/C, Am. Express
Prices: Moderate
Reservations: Suggested
Specialties: New American Cuisine

John Ash & Co. is moving, but do not despair, he won't be hard to find. A beautiful new building awaits his arrival at the exclusive Vintner's Inn. The move should be completed sometime in June of '87 and worried regulars can expect the same excellent cuisine they have come to know and love. John Ash is fast becoming one of America's new "hot" chefs and has been called a "culinary trendsetter." His "New American Cuisine" is complemented by an exemplary wine list, portions of which can be found for sale in the Wine Shop. The menu contains a stunning selection of appetizers and entrees prepared to perfection and beautifully presented with a French Nouvelle look. It's no wonder John Ash & Co. has earned a reputation as one of Northern California's finest.

191

ESTATE BOTTLED
ZINFANDEL
SONOMA VALLEY

HAYWOOD

A TABLE WINE GROWN, PRODUCED & BOTTLED
BY HAYWOOD WINERY • SONOMA • CALIFORNIA

Elegant and rich, this wine has intense berry flavors
with hints of spice and black pepper.

Food Pairing: Serve with spicy entrees, roast meats, tomato
sauces and blue cheeses.

Steak Paillards

Arrange very thin slices of *raw* top sirloin attractively on a plate. (Partially freeze first to facilitate cutting.)
Garnish with sprigs of watercress and following sauce.

Blend 5-10 seconds just until combined (*not* smooth):

¾ c. olive oil
½ c. chopped fresh parsley
½ c. drained capers
½ c. green olives
½ c. Dijon mustard
½ c. white wine vinegar
⅓ c. green peppercorns
12 cornichons
2 garlic cloves

Serves 1

Savory Vegetable Tart
in a Sweet Cornmeal Crust

Cornmeal crust:

½ c. butter at room temperature
½ c. sugar
1 c. yellow cornmeal
2 eggs at room temperature
1 t. salt
1½ c. all purpose flour

Blend butter and sugar until smooth. Add cornmeal, eggs, and

193

Savory Vegetable Tart (con't)

salt and beat until smooth. Add 1½ c. flour and beat in. Mixture should be soft and moist but can be rolled. Roll out and place in pie or tart pan.

Prebake in 350 degree oven for 7-8 minutes before filling. Note: this dough makes a wonderful little biscuit. Roll out and cut into desired shape. Bake approximately 20 minutes or until lightly brown.

Filling:

1 medium onion or 2 large leeks, finely minced
2 T. butter
¾ c. heavy cream
2 whole eggs
¾ c. very well baked winter squash, pureed
½ t. salt
1 t. honey
⅛ t. white pepper
big pinch each clove, cinnamon and nutmeg

Saute onion in butter until very soft but not brown. Cool and add to other ingredients and mix well. Pour into prepared tart shell and bake at 350 degrees for approximately 25 minutes or until filling is set and slightly puffed.

Top with very lightly blanched fresh vegetables in interesting patterns. Serve warm or at room temperature.

Makes 1 tart

Chevre Cheesecake

Crust:

1½ c. dry fresh breadcrumbs
⅓ c. sesame seeds
½ t. salt
½ c. ground pecans
2 T. melted butter

Combine all ingredients and pat into a 10" springform pan.

Filling:

½ c. shallots or green onions, minced
2 T. butter
1½ c. dry white wine
1 c. cream
2 lbs. chevre cheese (Boucheron or other flavorful
    bulk goat cheese)
1 lb. cream cheese (preferably natural without stabilizers)
3 eggs
1 t. salt
½t. ground white pepper

Saute shallots in butter until soft. Add white wine and reduce by half. Add ¾ c. cream and reduce by half again. Cool to room temperature. Beat remaining cream and rest of ingredients together until smooth. Pour into prepared pan above. Bake at 300 degrees for approximately 1 hour or until center of cake is softly set. Allow to cool before cutting.

Note: filling can be flavored with fresh herbs, minced green chili, minced smoked salmon, minced sun-dried tomato to taste. Cake is very rich so serve small slices. A fresh tomato coulis makes a good garnish.

Makes 1 10" cheesecake

Fresh Peach and Almond Tarte

Crust:

1 lb. flour
10 oz. butter
½ t. salt
½ c. sugar
1 egg

Blend flour, butter, salt and sugar until thoroughly blended, then add egg until it comes together.
This will make enough for about 3 tarts. Divide into 3 portions. This dough freezes well. Use 1 portion, roll out and fill tart shell (9" with removable bottom).

Filling:

½ lb. almond paste
½ lb. butter
6 oz. powdered sugar
1 lemon rind, grated
¾ c. ground toasted almonds
½ t. ground cardoman
3 oz. flour
1 egg

196

Fresh Peach and Almond Tarte (con't)

4 ripe Freestone peaches
¼-½ c. apricot preserves
toasted sliced almonds

Cream almond paste, butter and sugar, then add rind, almonds, cardoman and flour, then egg. Mix well. Spread a very thin layer of filling on bottom of shell.
Drop peaches in boiling water for about 1 minute. Peel and cut in half and remove pit. Place around edge of tart pan.

Bake at 375 degrees for 20 minutes or until golden brown. Filling should brown nicely and puff up. Cool.
Brush with apricot glaze: Warm apricot preserves with a little water. Strain.
Press toasted sliced almonds around edge of tart. Glaze edge of shell so nuts will stick.

Makes 1 tart

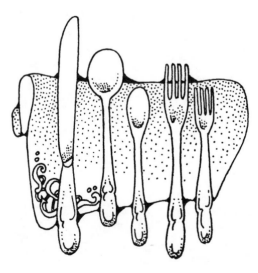

197

Vintners Inn

4350 Barnes Rd. • Santa Rosa, California 95401
(707) 575-7350 or (800) 421-2584

An old world atmosphere surrounds the Provence style Vintners Inn. A lushly land-scaped courtyard, with a fountain as the focal point of a four building complex, welcomes guests to the crossroads of Sonoma's wine country. There are forty-five over-sized rooms decorated in a French country motif, each with an elegant bath and dressing area. Also available are accommodations for executive conferences. Each weekend special events are planned, such as staged murder mysteries, art exhibits and special receptions. In June, John Ash & Co. will be moving his exciting restaurant to a newly finished building at the Inn. For exceptional hospitality, personal attention and John Ash & Co.'s fine food, join your hosts at the Vintners Inn.

Spanakopita

1 pkg. frozen filo dough
½ lb. plus 6 T. butter
2 T. flour
1 c. milk
¼ t. white pepper
⅛ t. nutmeg, freshly grated
1 onion, chopped
1 lb. fresh spinach leaves, chopped
3 eggs, beaten
1 c. Feta cheese, drained and crumbled

Thaw frozen filo in refrigerator overnight. Place package at room temperature 20 minutes before using.

Melt 2 T. of the butter until foamy. Whisk in flour; add milk in a slow stream whisking constantly until sauce thickens. Season with white pepper and nutmeg and set aside.

Saute onions in 2 T. butter until golden. Add 2 T. butter and the spinach, and saute until the spinach is soft and excess liquid has evaporated. Add spinach-onion mixture, eggs and cheese to sauce. Mix well.

Place filo on a flat working surface. Make 3 equal lengthwise cuts down the filo so that you will have 4 long stacks of dough. Cover with plastic wrap. Melt ½ lb. of butter.

Take 2 sheets of dough, placing 1 on top of the other. Using a pastry brush, brush well with melted butter. Place 1 T. of filling at lower left corner of filo strip. Fold lower left-hand corner across filling to right edge, as if folding a flag. Continue to fold in this manner to the top of the pastry strip.

Place triangle-shaped pastries on a cookie sheet. Bake in a 350 degree oven for 30 minutes or until golden. Serve while hot. Can be made ahead and frozen raw.

Makes about 3 dozen.

Chocolate Truffle Cake

7 oz. semisweet chocolate, crumbled
1 stick (4 oz.) unsalted butter
1 T. Grand Marnier
1 T. Meyers rum
1 t. vanilla
1 T flour
5 eggs, separated
¾ c. sugar
1-2 T. powdered sugar
garnish: orange zest

Place chocolate, 7 T. of the butter, Grand Marnier, rum, vanilla and flour in the top of a double boiler over hot water. Remove from heat as soon as ingredients melt. Mix well.
Whip egg yolks with half the sugar until cream colored. Add to chocolate mixture and blend well.

Whip egg whites and slowly add remaining sugar until firm. Gently blend chocolate mixture with egg white mixture.

Using reserved T. of butter, butter and flour a 10" springform cake pan. Line the bottom with a round of waxed paper or parchment. Pour batter into pan. Bake at 275 degrees for 1 hour, 20 minutes. Dust cooled cake with powdered sugar. Surface of cake will crumble when removed from pan and when cut.
Garnish each serving with a swirl of rum cream (recipe follows) and orange zest.

Rum Cream

1 pt. whipping cream
1 T. Meyers rum
1 t. vanilla
1 T. Grand Marnier
¾ c. sugar

Whip cream until it begins to thicken. Add rum, vanilla and Grand Marnier. Slowly add sugar until cream is stiff enough to put through a pastry tube.

Pavlova

Meringues:

4 egg whites
16 T. superfine sugar
2 t. vanilla

Preheat oven to 250 degrees. Oil 2 cookie sheets and line them
with brown or parchment paper. Beat egg whites until stiff but
not dry; add sugar a spoonful at a time. Beat well between each
addition. Add vanilla, beat until blended.
Draw two 8-10" circles on the brown or parchment paper. Spread
the meringue smoothly onto each circle.
Bake for 1 hour. Let dry in oven overnight.

Cream chantilly:

2 pts. heavy cream
1 T. vanilla
1 c. powdered sugar
1 T. Grand Marnier

Whip cream until slightly thickened. Add vanilla and 1 T. sugar,
beating continuously. Add the Grand Marnier and the remaining sugar. Beat until stiff.

Fruit filling:

6 kiwi fruits
2-3 baskets of strawberries

Peel and thinly slice the kiwi. Rinse, hull and thinly slice berries.
Place 1 meringue layer on a cake sheet, cover with cream chantilly and a layer of kiwi and berries. Top with a thin layer of cream
chantilly and the second layer of meringue. Frost with cream chantilly and arrange remaining berries and fruit on top.

Blue Cheese and Walnut Torta

1 lb. unsalted butter
1½ lb. cream cheese
8 oz. top quality blue cheese
2 c. toasted walnuts
Red Delicious apples or Bartlett pears

Bring butter and cream cheese to room temperature. Beat butter and cream cheese until light and fluffy. Line a mold with a large square of damp cheesecloth or plastic wrap; allow enough overhang to cover the open surface.

Place about 1½ c. of the cream cheese-butter mixture in the mold and press down smoothly over surface. Crumble in a layer of blue cheese, then cover with more of the cream cheese-butter mixture. Alternate layers of the cheeses, ending with the cream cheese-butter mixture. Pull sides of cloth or plastic wrap up to cover open surface and weight with a small plate or pan. Refrigerate at least 5 hours or up to 3 days, tightly wrapped.

Unmold onto a tray and press toasted walnuts into the surface, covering entirely.

Serve with thin slices of apple and pear that have been dipped in lemon water to keep from discoloring.

Serves 10-12

Fine Food & Wine On The Plaza

106 Matheson St. • Healdsburg, California 95448
(707) 433-3939
Hours: 11:30 a.m.-2:00 p.m. Lunch, Mon.-Sat.
(Saturday until 2:30 p.m.)
5:30-9:30 p.m. Dinner, Tues.-Thurs.
5:30-10:00 p.m. Dinner, Fri. and Sat.
10:30 a.m.-2:00 p.m. Brunch, Sunday
Credit Cards: Visa and M/C
Prices: Moderate
Reservations: Suggested
Specialties: California Grill featuring fresh produce, meat and
fish from Northern Sonoma County

The Jacob Horner Restaurant's motto is, "Fine food and wine on the Plaza," and it isn't a boast! Located downtown, Jacob Horner's faces a village green, ringed with bright specialty shops. The interior of the restaurant has a soothing quality assisted by the use of smooth woods, cool green plants, crisp linens and clean modern lines. A diverse menu offers the best in California Cuisine, using only the freshest vegetables, meats and fish from Northern Sonoma County. Jacob Horner's full bar and extensive Sonoma County wine list, combined with careful, attentive service, make dining here an epicurean delight.

205

Cold Peach Soup

1½ lbs. peaches, peeled, pitted and sliced
2 c. sour cream
1 c. orange juice
1 c. pineapple juice
½ c. dry sherry
2 T. lemon juice
sugar as needed

Puree peaches in food processor until smooth. Add all remaining ingredients except sugar and blend well. Pass soup through a fine strainer. Add sugar to taste. Serve chilled.

Serves 6-8

Eggplant Rolls

2 eggplants
2 t. salt
½ c. scallions, minced
olive oil
1¼ lbs. chunky plum tomato puree
1 t. dried basil
2 t. lemon juice
1 t. sugar
salt and pepper
10 slices prosciutto
8 oz. mozzarella, sliced
fresh basil for garnish

Peel eggplant and cut into ⅜" slices. Salt, drain and set aside. Preheat oven to 425 degrees. In a large skillet saute scallions in olive oil until soft, then add tomato puree, dried basil and simmer, covered, for 15 minutes. The mixture should not be too thick or watery. Strain and season with lemon juice, sugar, salt and pepper.
Rinse and dry eggplant slices. Lay them on a greased cookie sheet and bake 8 minutes, turn and bake another 8 minutes. Remove slices from sheet and cool.
To assemble: layer the eggplant with slice of prosciutto and mozzarella and gently roll. Serve at room temperature with some of the sauce under the roll and a small dollop over the top. Garnish with the fresh basil leaves.

Yield: 10 appetizers

Corn and Tomato Salad with Basil

16 ears white corn
8 large tomatoes, peeled, seeded, and chopped
¼ c. basil puree in olive oil
¼ c. olive oil
2 t. salt
2 t. black pepper

Cook corn in boiling water no longer than 4 minutes. Cool and cut kernels off cob. In a bowl combine corn with tomatoes, basil puree, oil, salt and pepper. Toss to mix and serve at room temperature.

Serves 8

Rabbit with Garlic Sauce

2 T. garlic, finely minced
¼ c. soft white breadcrumbs
¼ c. chicken fat
1 c. tomatoes, peeled, seeded and diced
1 c. chicken stock
1 c. dry white wine
1 3 lb. rabbit cut into 8 pieces

Bouquet garni:

¼ t. dried thyme
3 sprigs parsley
6 black peppercorns

Mix garlic with breadcrumbs. Cook in half the chicken fat about 2 minutes. Stir in tomatoes, stock, wine and bouquet garni. Bring to a boil and simmer for 30 minutes. Skim if necessary. In a large skillet brown rabbit in remaining chicken fat. Add browned rabbit to sauce and simmer covered for 40 minutes or until tender. Serve rabbit napped with some of the sauce.

Serves 4

Iced Puree of
Vegetables and Herbs

2 T. butter
1 lb. leeks, carefully washed and cut into slices
½ c. celery, coarsely chopped with leaves
¼ c. lemon juice
1 c. frozen peas
1 c. spinach, finely shredded
1 c. lettuce, finely shredded
8 c. chicken stock
2½ c. half-and-half
salt and pepper to taste
1 T. parsley, minced
1 T. mint leaves, minced

Melt butter in large heavy sauce pan over low heat. Add leeks, celery and lemon juice; cook until leeks are tender, stirring occasionally. Add peas, spinach and lettuce, then stir in stock and increase heat. Bring to boil and reduce heat and simmer until all vegetables are tender (about 10 minutes). Blend in half-and-half. Puree soup in blender or food processor and strain. Season with salt and pepper. Refrigerate overnight. Stir in parsley and mint just before serving.

Serves 6-8.

CLOS DU BOIS

Cabernet
Sauvignon

ALEXANDER VALLEY

90% Cabernet Sauvignon/10% Cabernet Franc

MADE & BOTTLED BY CLOS DU BOIS WINERY
HEALDSBURG, CA. USA•ALCOHOL 13.5% BY VOLUME•750 ML

Clos Du Bois' estate vineyards in Alexander Valley produce
Cabernets noted for their generous fruit and exceptional balance.
Two years of barrel aging in French and American oak
softens and adds complexity to the wine.

Food Pairing: Smooth and full-bodied, it complements
dark, rich meats.

Pork Satay with Peanut Sauce

Marinade:

¼ c. soy sauce
1½ T. sugar
1½ T. salad oil
2 cloves garlic, crushed
1 T. ginger root, grated
2½ lbs. pork loin, boned and thinly sliced

Sauce:

¼ c. lemon juice
¼ c. sugar
¼ c. soy sauce
1 T. ginger root, grated
3 cloves garlic, minced
¾ t. cayenne
¼ c. water
¾ c. chunky peanut butter

For the marinade, combine first 5 ingredients and add the sliced pork. Marinate for at least 2 hours.

For the sauce, heat all but peanut butter in a sauce pan over moderate heat. Stir until well combined and sugar has dissolved. Stir in peanut butter and allow to cool slightly.

Grill marinated pork slices and nap with the heated sauce.

Serves 12

JOHNSON'S
ALEXANDER VALLEY

ALEXANDER VALLEY

PINOT NOIR

PRODUCED AND BOTTLED BY

JOHNSON'S ALEXANDER VALLEY WINES
HEALDSBURG, SONOMA COUNTY, CALIFORNIA
ALCOHOL 12.5% BY VOLUME

A dark red color with a silky texture, this Pinot Noir
is excitingly full-bodied. There is a youthful, ripe cherry aroma
and a tantalizing full-fruit flavor with a tinge of herbaceousness.

This wine is excellent with lamb, veal and pork. Also, try it
with barbecued turkey.

STAGE A PICNIC
AND
BED & BREAKFAST

P.O. Box 536 • Geyserville, California 95441
(707) 857-3619

What a way to see the wine country and relive the colorful history of Napa Valley—touring by stage! Authentic horse drawn stages, driven by experienced and historically knowledgeable Dick and Shellie Dilworth, transport you through time. You'll learn the culture of the vineyards, hear tales from long ago and see the winemaking process at a major facility and two more intimate, family owned and operated wineries. There are two tours each day—one in the morning, ending with a sumptuous picnic, and the second one in the afternoon which begins with a picnic at the Trentadue Winery. The country air and the aroma of the taste-tempting delights those picnic baskets hold will sharpen any palate. Fresh salads, succulent fruits, locally made sausages, cheeses and smoked meats with award winning breads and other homemade specialties are stuffed into roomy picnic baskets by Rosalie Hope of the Hope-Merrill House and the Hope-Bosworth House. Come take a ride and experience the wine country at its best.

213

Torta Rustica

4 T. butter
2 c. spinach, washed, well drained and chopped
salt and pepper
grating of fresh nutmeg
4 eggs
1 recipe brioche, made a day ahead (recipe follows)
2 lbs. mozzarella cheese, thinly sliced
1 c. ricotta cheese
2 lbs. prosciutto, thinly sliced
2 2½ oz. cans pimentos, drained
1 egg, mixed with water
1 c. homemade mayonnaise mixed with 2 T. Dijon mustard

Heat 2 T. of the butter in a medium frying pan, add spinach and saute over low heat until all the moisture has been cooked out, about 30 minutes. Season with the salt, pepper and nutmeg. Meanwhile, make two 2 egg omlettes in an 8" pan using the remaining butter and set aside. Roll out half the brioche dough on a lightly floured pastry cloth to a 10" round about 1" thick. Line an 8" springform pan with the dough. There should be about a 1" overlap at the rim. Line the dough bottom and sides with the mozzarella. Lay in one omelette. Cover with ½ c. of the spinach and smooth with the back of a spoon. Repeat with the ricotta cheese. Cover with a 1" layer of prosciutto, putting several big chunks of pimento at various intervals. Cover with a ½" layer of mozzarella and the remaining ricotta. Repeat prosciutto and cheese layers ending with an omelette covered with a spinach layer and a 1" thick layer of mozzarella. The layering should fill the pan completely so it heaps up in the middle above the rim. Preheat oven to 400 degrees. Roll out the rest of the dough to form a 9" circle and place on top of the torta. Pinch the 2 pieces together all around making a nicely fluted edge. Put 3 short cuts

214

Torta Rustica (con't)

in the top. You can use some of the leftover dough to make creative cutouts for the top. Brush the torta with the egg mixture and bake for 30 minutes. Check after 20 minutes; if top is browning too rapidly cover with foil. Let cool in pan. Wrap in foil until ready to serve. Undo the springform pan, leaving the torta on the base. Place it on a large platter and garnish all around with radish roses, cornichons, pickled mushrooms and parsley. Serve cut into wedges with the homemade mayonnaise and mustard combination.

Serves 10-12

Brioche Dough

½ c. warm water
1 pkg. yeast
2 T. sugar
1 T. salt
1 c. butter, softened
6 eggs
4½ c. flour, sifted before measuring

Mix all ingredients and 3 c. of the flour. Beat for 4 minutes at medium speed of mixer. Add the rest of the flour and continue to beat for 2 minutes more. Cover the dough with plastic wrap or towel and let rise for 2 hours. Punch down and refrigerate overnight.

Makes enough for 1 Torta Rustica

Muffaletta

Salad Filling:

1½ c. stuffed green olives, chopped
1 c. black olives, chopped
⅓ c. olive oil
⅓ c. parsley, chopped
4 oz. pimento, chopped
1 T. anchovy paste, from a tube
1 T. capers
1 clove garlic
1 T. fresh oregano, or 1 t. dried
¼ t. pepper

Sandwiches:

¼ lb. salami, sliced
½ lb. provolone, sliced
½ lb. mortadella, sliced
1½ lb. round sour dough loaf of bread

To prepare the salad filling, chop all the salad ingredients in a food processor and refrigerate several days before assembling the sandwiches.

To assemble, drain the salad and reserve the liquid. Slice the top off the loaf and brush bread with drained liquid. Pat half the salad mixture into the bottom of the bread. Layer as follows: mortadella, provolone, salami, provolone and mortadella. The remaining salad goes inside the top part of the bread. Place the top on and tie securely. Wrap it well and weight it down in the refrigerator for up to 1 hour. Slice and serve.

Serves 12

(A Favorite New Orleans Style Sandwich)

216

THE CAMPBELL RANCH INN

1475 Canyon Road • Geyserville, California 95441
(707) 857-3476

Expect personalized service far from the maddening crowd when you stay with Mary Jane and Jerry Campbell at their secluded hilltop Inn surrounded with spectacular views of rolling vineyards and abundantly flowered gardens. The Campbell Ranch Inn has three spacious rooms filled with the aroma of Mary Jane's fresh flowers and succulent seasonal fruits. Two of the rooms have private balconies with breathtaking views of the countryside. A delicious country breakfast is served on the sun-bathed terrace in the spring and summer. When you are finished, enjoy a brisk game of tennis on the professional court or just lounge around the pool and hot tub spa. Be sure to bring your camera for the hikes and bicycle rides to capture the panoramic beauty of the valley for long lasting memories.

217

Campbell Ranch Inn Egg Puff

¼ lb. margarine
1 lb. fresh mushrooms, diced
10 extra-large eggs
1 lb. Monterey Jack cheese, shredded
1 pt. creamed cottage cheese
½ c. white flour
1 t. baking powder
½ t. salt

In a large frying pan, melt margarine, and set aside to cool. Place diced mushrooms in cooled margarine and stir until completely coated. In a large mixer bowl, beat eggs until well blended. Add all ingredients and stir. Place 9 well-greased ramekins on cookie sheet. Pour in batter (about ¾ c. in each). Bake in a preheated 350 degree oven until golden brown on top or knife inserted comes out clean, approximately 45 minutes. Take 1 ramekin out at a time and run the blade of the knife around the edge to remove. Serve immediately; or to freeze place puff on cooling rack. Repeat for all 9 puffs. Place rack of puffs into freezer. When solidly frozen, remove from freezer and wrap individually in foil. The section of foil which will touch the top of the puff should be well greased with margarine for easy removal. Put all 9 wrapped puffs into a plastic bag and return to freezer.

To reheat place the desired number of puffs you need on a cookie sheet. Place in a 400 degree oven and bake for 1 hour. Unwrap and place on a warm plate to serve.

Serves 9

Chocolate Whipped Cream Cake

Cake:

1 pkg. Betty Crocker's Super Moist
   Chocolate Fudge Cake Mix
1 pt. whipping cream
2 T. sugar
1 t. vanilla

Frosting:

1 sm. pkg. Nestles' chocolate chips
¼ lb. butter
1 extra-large egg
1 c. powdered sugar

Bake the cake according to instructions on package. *Do not over-bake!* Cool on wire racks. When cool, slice each layer in half horizontally to make 4 thin layers. Whip the cream with the sugar and vanilla. On cake stand or serving plate (or on waxed paper if you're going to freeze cake) place first layer. Spread about ⅓ of the whipped cream to cover the layer. Repeat with all the layers but do not frost the top and sides. In top of double boiler, over hot, not boiling water, melt chocolate chips and butter. Let cool, then beat in the egg and powdered sugar. Whip with mixer until light and fluffy. Frost the sides and top of the cake. Use any leftover frosting to decorate the cake with a pastry tube. If you are making ahead and freezing, do not decorate. Freeze the cake solidly and then wrap airtight in foil. Freeze the remaining frosting in a jar. The day you serve the cake, thaw and decorate.

Serves 16

Honey Wheat Bread

1½ c. boiling water
1 c. rolled oats
¾ c. honey
2 T. butter, softened
2 t. salt
1 pkg. dry yeast
2 c. lukewarm water
1 c. 7-grain cereal
3 c. whole wheat flour
4 c. white flour

Pour boiling water over the oats and let stand for 30 minutes. Add honey, soft butter and salt. Dissolve the yeast in the warm water and add to the oats. Stir in the 7-grain cereal and the whole wheat flour. Then add the white flour to make a medium soft dough. Turn onto a floured board; knead until the dough is smooth and elastic (about 10 minutes). Place dough in greased bowl and turn once to coat top. Cover with a damp towel and let rise until double in bulk. Knead again. Divide into 6 equal portions. Shape into small loaves and place in 6 greased 5" x 3" x 2" foil loaf pans. Place the pans on a large cookie sheet, cover with a damp towel and let rise until doubled again. Preheat oven to 400 degrees. Bake 5 minutes and lower the heat to 350 degrees. Bake 25-30 minutes or until the loaves sound hollow when tapped. Remove the bread from the pans onto a wire rack for cooling. Brush the tops with melted butter. Serve warm, or wrap in foil and when completely cool, freeze for later use. To serve the frozen bread, thaw in foil and warm in 140 degree oven for 45 minutes to an hour. Almost tastes freshly made!

Yield: 6 loaves

Rice Krispie Cookies

6 c. Rice Krispies cereal
1 c. white Karo corn syrup
1 c. sugar
1½ c. peanut butter
1 small pkg. Nestles' chocolate chips, melted

Measure out a scant 6 c. of cereal into a large bowl and set aside. In a sauce pan, bring to boil the syrup and sugar; add the peanut butter and mix well. Pour this over the cereal and mix thoroughly. Spoon into a 9" x 12" pan and press smooth with fingertips. In top of double boiler, melt chocolate chips and spread over cereal mixture. Cut into squares while still warm. Great for picnics or mailing to your college kids, and they freeze beautifully.

Yield: 36 cookies

Sour Cream Coffee Cake

Crumb filling:

¾ c. dried bread crumbs
½ c. flour
½ c. butter
⅓ c. sugar
1½ t. cinnamon
½ t. nutmeg
1 c. or more walnuts, or any combination of nuts,
  finely ground

Coffee Cake:

1½ c. sugar
¾ c. margarine
3 extra large eggs
1½ c. sour cream
1½ t. baking powder
1½ t. baking soda
1½ t. vanilla
3 c. white flour

Preheat the oven to 350 degrees. Grease a 10" tube pan and set aside for later use. In a small bowl of mixer, with speed on low, beat together the first 6 ingredients of the crumb recipe. When the mixture is well blended, stir in the nuts with fork. Set aside for later use.

In a large mixing bowl beat sugar and margarine until light and fluffy. Add the remaining ingredients, scraping the sides of the bowl often. Beat at a medium speed for 3 minutes. Spread ⅓ of the batter into the tube pan. Sprinkle with ⅓ of the crumb mixture. Repeat 2 more times. Bake 55-60 minutes or until toothpick inserted comes out clean. Do not overbake! This coffee cake freezes beautifully.

Serves 12-15

SONOMA COAST/ RUSSIAN RIVER

GUALALA

ST. ORRES

WHALE WATCH INN

THE ESTATE

BAREFOOT CELLARS

'BOUT TIME RESTAURANT

RAFORD HOUSE

RIDENHOUR RANCH HOUSE INN

KORBEL

HEALDSBURG

Pacific Ocean

1

JENNER

GUERNEVILLE

RIVER'S END

River Road

101

1

INN AT THE TIDES

BODEGA BAY

12

PELICAN LANDING

SANTA ROSA

VALLEY FORD

SONOMA COAST VILLA

PETALUMA

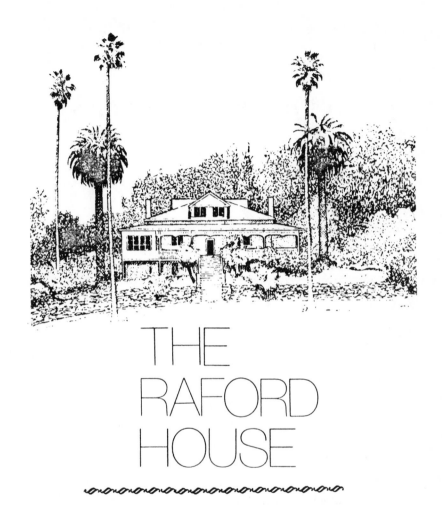

THE RAFORD HOUSE

10630 Wohler Road • Healdsburg, California 95448
(707) 887-9573

Originally designed to be the main residence of a 400 acre hops ranch, The Raford House was built in the 1880's by Raford W. Peterson. One hundred years later Alan Baitinger and Beth Foster bought the Sonoma County Historical Landmark with the idea of transforming it into a Bed and Breakfast Inn. In June of 1981 the work was completed and the doors were opened for the first time. The inviting guest rooms are tastefully furnished in period antiques and guaranteed conducive to a relaxing stay. In the morning plan a day of exploration while you savor a complimentary breakfast of warm rolls, fresh baked breads, seasonal fruit and homemade jams and jellies. Your plans could include tours of the local wineries, a visit to some of the historical points of interest, or the taste tempting wares at any of the intriguing restaurants. After a busy day relax and enjoy the view from the spacious front porch or stroll over grassy patios while you drink in the fragrance of over one hundred rose bushes.

225

Al's Honey Bran Muffins

1 c. bran cereal
¼ c. milk
¼ c. honey
2 eggs
¼ c. butter, softened
1 T. pure vanilla
¾ c. raisins
1 c. flour
2½ t. baking powder
¼ t. salt
½ c. brown sugar
⅓ c. shortening
2 T. honey

Preheat oven to 375 degrees. Combine cereal, milk and ¼ c. honey and let stand 10 minutes. Beat in eggs, butter and vanilla. Then mix in raisins. In a large bowl combine flour, baking powder and salt. Add the bran mixture, mixing just until dry ingredients are moistened and set aside. Mix the brown sugar, shortening and 2 T. honey together and heavily coat a 12 muffin tin with it. Fill each muffin cup ⅔ full with the batter and bake 15-18 minutes.

Yield: 1 dozen muffins.

Hint: Push raisins to bottom and when the muffins are done remove immediately and turn upside down so raisin and coating will be on top.

Prickly Pear Cactus Jelly

5 lbs. cactus meat
½ c. water
½ c. lemon juice
1½ pkgs. dry pectin
6 c. sugar

Cut prickly pear cactus in half and scoop out meat. In a large kettle add the cactus meat and water. Simmer 10 minutes and press out the juice through a jelly bag or cotton flour sacks, adding another layer of cloth for each strain. With 5 cups of liquid, including the ½ cup lemon juice, add the pectin and bring to a boil. Slowly add the sugar and return to a rolling boil. Stir 2 minutes, pour into prepared canning jars and seal.

Yield: Approximately 10 cups

J. PEDRONCELLI

Sonoma County
Fumé Blanc

Sauvignon Blanc

DRY CREEK VALLEY

PRODUCED AND BOTTLED BY J. PEDRONCELLI WINERY
GEYSERVILLE, SONOMA COUNTY, CALIFORNIA
ALCOHOL 12.5% BY VOLUME

The nose of this Fume Blanc has an interestingly full, lush, smoky,
round, lemony, melon aroma. On the palate, the wine is smooth
and big-bodied with lemon and grass flavors.
The finish is rich, long and spicy.

This is a perfect wine to enjoy by itself and is great with
grilled fish, cracked crab, smoked meats and lighter pasta dishes.

Ridenhour
Ranch House Inn

12850 River Road • Guerneville, California 95446
(707) 887-1033

Nestled amidst lush greenery and towering redwoods, the Ridenhour Ranch House Inn beckons the traveler. It was built in 1906 of native heart redwood by Louis E. Ridenhour, and has been painstakingly transformed into a unique country Inn by Bob and Martha Satterthwaite. Each of the seven rooms (four with private baths) are filled with carefully chosen English and American antiques to enhance the serenity of country living. The informal grounds provide inviting paths to explore the surrounding forest or you can relax in the oak-shaded hot tub. In the evening sip wine in front of the brick fireplace while enjoying views of the majestic redwoods. Every morning savor an appetizing breakfast of various breads, seasonal fruits, cheese, freshly ground coffee, English and herbal teas.

Gravenstein Applesauce

12-14 Gravenstein apples or any tart apple, peeled and sliced
¾ c. sugar (approximate according to tartness of apples)
⅓ c. orange juice
⅔ c. Port wine
½ c. water
½-¾ t. cinnamon
grated rind of 1 orange
dash of salt

Combine all ingredients in a large stock pot. Bring to a boil and simmer until apples are soft and mushy, stirring frequently. Cool and serve.

Refrigerator Bran Muffins

3 c. whole bran cereal
1 c. boiling water
2 eggs, lightly beaten
2 c. buttermilk
½ c. salad oil
1 c. raisins, currants, chopped pitted dates, chopped pitted
  prunes or any combination of dried fruits
2½ t. soda
½ t. salt
1 c. sugar
2¾ c. unbleached, enriched flour

In a large bowl, combine cereal with boiling water, stirring to
moisten. Set aside and cool; add eggs, buttermilk, oil and fruit;
blend well. In a separate bowl mix together the soda, salt, sugar
and flour then stir in the bran mixture. (At this point you may
tightly cover and refrigerate for as long as 2 weeks, baking muffins at your convenience; stir batter to evenly distribute fruit before
using.)
To bake, spoon batter into greased 2½" diameter muffin cups.
(Fill each about ¾ full.) Bake in 425 degree oven for about 20
minutes or until tops spring back when lightly touched. Serve hot.

Yields 2 dozen

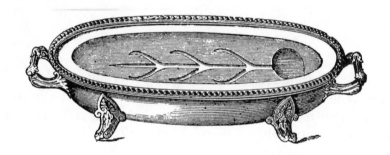

ᾯhe ᾮstate

13555 Highway 116 • Guerneville, California 95446
(707) 869-9093

Indulge yourself in a gracious style of living at The Estate. The luxurious mansion was originally designed to be a paragon of elegant living for the discriminating. Ten spacious suites adorned with works of art and antiques, coupled with personalized attention from a staff eager to please, provide the perfect background to experience a lifestyle of a time gone by. A hearty country breakfast is served each morning and hors d'oeuvres with wine each evening. Swim in the heated pool, relax in the spa, or stroll along the beaches and discover the unique forms of sea creatures that inhabit the tidepools. Visit a winery, renew yourself at a nearby mudbath and in the evening enjoy local cabarets, dancing, exquisite restaurants and repertory theatre. All this and much more await your pleasure at The Estate.

233

Caviar Pie

6 hard boiled eggs, finely chopped
2 T. mayonnaise
1 medium red onion, finely chopped, drained on
  paper towel for 30 minutes
⅔ c. sour cream
8 oz. cream cheese at room temperature
3½ or 4 oz. jar black caviar
sliced lemons and fresh parsley for garnish

Line the bottom of a 8½" or 9" springform pan with a waxed
paper circle and butter it. Place the hard boiled eggs mixed with
mayonnaise in bottom of pan. Place the onions on top of egg
layer. Blend sour cream and cream cheese until smooth. Spread
carefully over the onion layer and chill 1 hour. Remove side of
pan carefully and invert onto glass serving platter. Drain the
caviar on paper towels for 10 minutes and arrange over top.
Garnish with lemon slices and parsley. Serve with crackers and
Champagne.   *Yield: 16-18 appetizer portions*

Persimmon Pancakes

1 egg
1 c. buttermilk
2 T. salad oil
1 c. all-purpose flour
1 T. sugar
1 t. baking powder
½ t. baking soda
½ t. salt
1 c. persimmon pulp
½ c. walnuts (optional)
2 t. cinnamon

Beat egg and add remaining ingredients. Mix until well blended.

Persimraon Pancakes (con't)

Pour batter onto hot griddle. Turn when bubbles appear on surface. Cook to desired doneness and serve dusted with powdered sugar and maple syrup.

Serves 4

Blackberry Clafouti

Crust:

1½ c. all-purpose flour
½ c. unsalted butter, chilled and cut into pieces
¼ t. salt
¼ c. cold water

Filling:

3 c. fresh blackberries

Topping:

4 large eggs
1 c. plus 8 t. sugar
¾ c. unsalted butter, melted
¼ c. all-purpose flour
1 t. vanilla

Grease an 11" tart pan with removable bottom. For crust, combine flour, butter and salt. Cut butter into flour with 2 knives until it resembles a coarse meal. Add the water and mix until dough comes away from the sides of the bowl. Wrap in plastic and chill for 30 minutes. Preheat the oven to 350 degrees.
Roll the pastry into a 12" circle and place in the prepared tart pan. Fill with the berries, and set aside.
For the topping, mix together the eggs, sugar, butter, flour and vanilla. Pour over the berries. Bake in the lower half of the oven for 1 hour. Serve warm or cooled with whipped cream or creme fraiche.* It's best if it is eaten the same day.

Serves 8

*See Glossary

RESTAURANT

Main St. • Guerneville, California 94562
(707) 869-2844
Hours: 11:00 a.m.-3:00 p.m. Lunch, Seven Days a Week
5:30-10:00 p.m. Dinner, Sun.-Thurs.
5:30-11:00 p.m. Dinner, Fri. and Sat.
Credit Cards: All Major
Prices: Moderate
Reservations: Suggested
Specialties: Pasta, Veal, Seafood and Luncheon Salads

Set among the picturesque mud flat beaches and clapboard cabins of the Russian River is the "cleanest most interesting bar and restaurant on the river." The 'Bout Time Restaurant is a step above the average with a delightful bright green and crisp white decor and lots of windows to accentuate that airy feeling of "patio" dining. Their motto, "The Customer is King," typifies their attitude toward timely, attentive service and quality ingredients—for here food is king, too! The regular menu features pasta, veal and seafood dishes, with innovative luncheon salads and daily specials. To complement these delicious meals there is a full service bar and every Sunday night live jazz.

237

Deep Fried Brie

8 oz. wedge of Brie cheese
1 c. flour
2-3 eggs, well beaten
1 c. bread crumbs
oil for frying
Carrs water crackers
seedless green and red grapes

Do not remove white rind on cheese. Coat cheese in flour and shake off excess. Place in egg mixture and then coat evenly with bread crumbs. In a skillet heat enough oil to completely cover wedge and fry for no longer than 1 minute (360 degrees is best temperature). Remove immediately to serving plate and garnish with crackers and grapes. (For more than 4 people, prepare more wedges of the same size, as larger pieces do not tend to soften properly.)

Serves 2-4

Chocolate Decadence

1¾ lbs. semisweet chocolate
1 shot of brandy
½ lb. butter
¼ c. superfine sugar
1⅓ c. half-and-half
5 eggs, lightly beaten

Place chocolate, brandy, butter, sugar and half and half in top of double boiler and heat until well blended and smooth. Remove from heat and cool slightly. Add lightly beaten eggs and stir until well blended. Line bottom of 9" round cake pan with wax paper and coat sides with vegetable oil or margarine. Pour in chocolate mixture. Place cake pan on cookie sheet containing ½" layer of water and bake in a preheated oven at 275 degrees for 2 hours. Cool completely and refrigerate. Serve topped with whipped cream.

Serves 8-10.

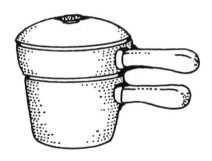

16702 Coast Highway • Valley Ford, California 94972
(707) 876-3225
Hours: 5:00-10:00 p.m. Dinner, Wed.-Sat.
12:00 noon-4:00 p.m. Sunday Lunch
4:00-10:00 p.m. Sunday Dinner
Credit Cards: All Major
Prices: Expensive
Reservations: Recommended
Specialties: French and California

*Thrill to sybaritic pleasures at the exclusive Sonoma Coast Villa. Cradled in the
bosom of gently rounded hills, the incomparable red tile and stucco Inn combines
the ultimate in sophistication with relaxed country squire living. Six villas, with
amenities too numerous to mention, are arranged around a jewel-like swimming pool.
Activities abound for pleasure-seeking guests. Enjoy swimming, sunning or strolling
along sandy beaches, tennis, golf, trapshooting, horseback riding or wine tastings and
cooking sessions (by appointment) led by Chef Grant Pattison, plus the many other
activities available to visitors to the Sonoma Coast. The Blue Boar Restaurant has
become a special place at the Villa. Stained and leaded glass, wall tapestries, terra
cotta floors, fabric-covered screens and vaulted ceilings set a romantic mood in the
carefully composed dining room. An extensive wine list, referred to by some as the
finest in California, complements unsurpassed gourmet cooking and professional service. In short, few rivals can equal the Sonoma Coast Villa and The Blue Boar Inn.*

Potted Shrimp Blue Boar

10 T shallots, finely chopped
½ c. dried tarragon leaves
pinch of cayenne
10 T. butter
1 lb. cooked shrimp
salt

Saute the shallots, tarragon and cayenne in 5 tablespoons of butter without browning. Remove from the heat and cool to lukewarm. Whip in the remaining butter and, when the mixture is creamy, add the shrimp, which should be at room temperature. Mix well so that the shrimp is well coated with butter. Place in a jar, cover and refrigerate for several hours.

Arrange on a bed of shredded lettuce, sprinkle liberally with oil and vinegar dressing, garnish with lemon wedges and serve with toast.

Serves 4

*This variation of the traditional English appetizer
evolved in the Blue Boar kitchen through
cooperative suggestions of the staff.*

Goat Cheese Salad

4 rounds goat cheese (about 2" thick)
4 oz. goat meat, cut into strips
1 head butter lettuce (rinse and pat dry)
4 T. walnuts, chopped
1 tomato, cut in quarters
1 bunch watercress

Place goat cheese on a lightly oiled baking sheet. Place strips of goat meat on top. Bake in preheated 400 degree oven for 4 minutes (until the cheese is bubbling). Meanwhile, toss the lettuce and walnut dressing (recipe follows) and place on 4 cold salad plates. Place 1 T. chopped walnuts in the center of each salad. Add tomatoes and watercress. Place goat cheese rounds on top.

Serves 4

242

Sea Bass Blue Boar

1 shallot, chopped
6 mushrooms, sliced
1 T. butter
2 sea bass fillets
1 c. white wine
¾ c. water
pinch of thyme
½ bay leaf
roux*
3 T. cream or half and half
salt and pepper
1 tomato, peeled and diced

In a pan, saute shallots and mushrooms in butter. Add sea bass, wine and water. Add thyme and bay leaf. Cover pan and simmer for about 20 minutes. Remove fish, reduce broth and pour hot broth into cold roux. Stir. Add cream, salt, pepper and tomato. Pour sauce over fish and serve immediately.

Makes 1 large or 2 small servings
*See Glossary

Red Cabbage Blue Boar

3 lbs. red cabbage, finely sliced
1 large apple, peeled, diced
4 oz. butter, melted
2 oz. red wine vinegar
salt and pepper
4 oz. sugar
12 oz. chicken broth

Combine all ingredients in a stock pot and cook over medium flame, stirring occasionally until soft.

Serves 4

243

Walnut Dressing

½ c. walnut oil
1 t. French mustard
3 T. champagne vinegar
1 T. madeira
¼ c. walnuts, chopped
salt and pepper

Prepare dressing by whisking the walnut oil into the mustard. Add vinegar, madeira, chopped walnuts, salt and pepper.

Serves 4

Blue Boar Cheddar Cheese Salad

3 parts mayonnaise
1 part buttermilk
1 part finely shredded sharp cheddar cheese
dash of Worcestershire sauce
pinch of cayenne
touch of red wine
vinegar to taste
salt and pepper

Mix ingredients and chill. Aim at a mixture that will make the dressing of such a consistency as to coat well the lettuce to be used for the salad. Use a mix of shredded iceberg and romaine lettuce, well chilled. After tossing in dressing serve garnished with cherry tomatoes, chopped green onions and grated cheddar cheese sprinkled over top in amounts desired.

New York Pepper Steak
With Pepper Sauce

2 t. cracked pepper
1 t. salt
4 New York steaks
1 t. oil
1 T. butter
2 T. cognac
½ pt. brown sauce*
4 T. soft butter
1 T. cognac
1 t. green peppercorns

Apply freshly cracked pepper and salt to both sides of each steak. Using a heavy frying pan, heat oil and butter. Add steaks and cook until rare or medium rare. Remove steaks and discard oil and butter mixture. Replace steaks and flambe with 2 T. cognac. Remove the steaks and keep warm. In same frying pan add brown sauce to the steak juices and cognac. Bring to boil. Gradually add soft butter (shake pan over flame to melt the butter). Add 1 T. cognac and green peppercorns. Pour sauce over steaks and serve immediately.

Serves 4

*See Glossary

The Inn at the Tides

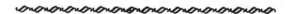

800 Highway 1 • Bodega Bay, California 94923
(707) 875-2751

Bodega Bay proudly displays its newest arrival, the contemporary Inn at the Tides. The Inn boasts convenient, comfortable accommodations with a host of thoughtful amenities, including a Continental breakfast. The suite-sized rooms overlook the quaint fishing village of Bodega Bay and the blue vistas of the Pacific beyond. When you check in be sure to make reservations for a magnificent dinner in the Bayview Room. Chef John Meidinger, with the assistance of an eager staff, titillates a sea-air sharpened appetite with innovative delicacies creatively presented. You'll relish the Deep Fried Soft Shell Crabs with Chili Oil, Swordfish Saute with Two Sauces, Scallop and Prawn Brochette with Tomato Concasse, Medallions of Beef El Gran Rey, Mini Coho Salmon Saute Burroso—the list goes on and on, with each entree more beautiful and delicious than the last. Plan a visit soon to the memorable Inn at the Tides.

Tortellini Salad

1 head radicchio
1 head escarole
6 oz. tortellini*
pesto salad dressing (recipe follows)
2 oz. dry Vella Jack cheese, grated
2 oz. pine nuts, roasted (pignolias)
basil leaves

Remove outer leaves of radicchio and soak in cold water. Clean and tear into bite-size pieces remaining radicchio leaves and escarole leaves; let these crisp in cold water. Cook tortellini in boiling salted water for 10-12 minutes or until al dente. Rinse and quickly cool. After draining, toss tortellini in pesto salad dressing. Assemble salad as follows:

1) Pat dry outer leaves of radicchio head and line plates to form a bowl within lining of salad plates; 2) strain all water from prepared escarole and radicchio and place inside radicchio leaf "bowl"; 3) top with 4-5 tortellini, then grated cheese, then pine nuts; 4) drizzle salad dressing over entire salad and garnish with 2 basil leaves.

Serves 4

*Tortellini is found in the freezer section of the supermarket. Just follow instructions on the package.

Pesto Salad Dressing

½ c. basil leaves
2 oz. olive oil
½ T. red wine vinegar
½ T. pine nuts
1 t. garlic, minced
1 t. Parmesan cheese, grated

In mixing bowl or food processor combine ingredients and puree. Salt and pepper to taste.

Yield: 1¾ cups

Radicchio and Limestone Lettuce Salad

1 head radicchio
1 head limestone lettuce
1 egg yolk
⅓ c. red wine vinegar
½ t. Dijon mustard
1 c. olive oil
salt and black pepper
chopped parsley (optional)

Radicchio is a sweet red Italian cabbage, and limestone lettuce is a type of bibb lettuce grown in limestone-enhanced soil. Rinse salad lettuces dry and break into bite sized pieces. Toss with dressing; top with chopped parsley, if desired.

Dressing:

In bowl or food processor add egg yolk, vinegar and mustard. Start machine and slowly drizzle oil into bowl until all is incorporated. Season with salt and pepper to taste.

Serves 6-8

Pork Scallopine Sauce Robert

1 center cut pork loin
flour
olive oil
½ t. shallots, minced
2 T. white wine
½ t. lemon juice
1 T. demi glace*
½ t. butter
salt and pepper

Cut pork loin in 2 oz. medallions. Place between 2 pieces of wax paper or plastic wrap and pound with flat part of heavy meat cleaver until very flat (about ⅛" thick). Use 2 to 3 of these scallopine per person. Dredge in flour and place in hot saute pan with enough olive oil to coat. Cook each side for no more than 30 seconds. Remove meat to serving plate. Pour off excess grease from frying pan. Put pan back on fire, add minced shallots, cook until brown and add white wine and lemon juice. Reduce by ⅓ and add demi glace and butter. Season to taste with salt and pepper. Pour sauce over cooked scallopine.

Serves 1

*See Glossary

Poached Pear Italiano

1 Bosc or Comice pear, peeled
water
red wine
1 c. sugar
peel of 1 lemon
spumoni ice cream
chocolate sauce
caramel sauce

Immerse pear in a pan of half water and half red wine. Add sugar
and the lemon peel. Bring to a simmer for 5 minutes. Let cool
in liquid. When cool slice the bottom so pear will stand upright.
With a spoon scoop out bottom, removing seeds and forming a
pocket, which you will fill with spumoni ice cream. Place on plate
and surround with chocolate sauce. Drizzle some caramel sauce
over the pear.   *Serves 1*

New York Style Cheesecake

2 eggs
½ c. sugar
6 oz. heavy cream
6 oz. cream cheese
1 lemon, juiced
1½ c. sour cream
2 T. sugar
½ t. vanilla extract

Beat eggs thoroughly, add sugar, heavy cream, cream cheese and
lemon juice. Pour the batter into a greased springform pan and
bake in 350 degree oven for 20 minutes. Cool for 5 minutes. Pour
the sour cream sweetened with the sugar and vanilla extract over
the cake. Bake the cake in a 475 degree oven for 5 minutes.
Chill before serving and accompany with some fresh fruit soaked
in rum.

Serves 10-12

PELICAN LANDING

1400 Coast Highway 1 • Bodega Bay, California 95462
(707) 875-2774
Hours: 11:30 a.m.-9:30 p.m. Lunch and Dinner
10:00 a.m.-1:00 p.m. Sat. and Sun. Brunch
Closed Tues. and Wed.
Credit Cards: M/C, Visa
Prices: Moderate
Reservations: Suggested
Specialties: Seafood, Pasta and Meats

The nautical themed Pelican Landing offers a cool, casual dining experience overlooking Bodega Bay. Polished brass, warm woods and a menu that insists on the freshest ingredients and "made from scratch preparations" featuring the bounty of the local waters and far away ports, combine to make a classic dining experience. Start with a steaming bowl of chowder, freshly shucked oysters, Calamari Ceveche, or fragrant "buckets" of steamed clams. Follow with light entrees like the classic Hangtown Fry, Seafood Salad on grilled French bread or fresh pasta with creamy or piquant sauces. For dessert try the chocoholics' delight, Gateau Mocha or a rich and smooth Rum Chocolate Mousse. Then go tell your friends you have "discovered" another great place to dine.

253

Steamed Clams

1½ lbs. Manila clams, well rinsed
water
white wine
dash of Tabasco
dash of Worcestershire sauce
1 t. green onion, chopped
1 t. parsley, chopped
1 t. garlic, chopped
1 T. butter

Place the clams in a 10" skillet. Add enough water to cover the clams ½ way. Add enough white wine to cover them ¼ more. Add Tabasco, Worcestershire sauce, green onion, parsley, garlic and butter. Cover and cook until clams open.

Serves 2

Linguine and Baby Clams

8 oz. linguine
1 T. butter
1 T. garlic, minced
1 small can baby clams with liquid
white wine
1 T. parsley, chopped

Cook pasta so it still has color. In a 10" skillet melt the butter; add garlic and saute until lightly toasted. Add the linguine and the baby clams with their liquid.

Finish with white wine to taste and garnish with parsley. You should have enough broth to form a little pool around the pasta.

Serves 2

River's End

Highway 1 • Jenner, California 95450
(707) 865-2484
Hours: 5:00-9:30 p.m. Dinner, Wed.-Sat.
4:00-9:00 p.m. Dinner, Sun.
11:00 a.m.-4:00 p.m. Lunch, Sat.
10:00 a.m.-3:00 p.m. Brunch, Sun
Closed on Mon. and Tues.
Closed during Dec., Jan. and Feb.
Credit Cards: Visa and M/C
Prices: Moderate
Reservations: Suggested
Specialties: International Cuisine with a German Influence

Intimate dining overlooking the ocean and the scenic Russian River await you at The River's End Restaurant and Tavern. In a rustic dining room accented with warm, homey woods, bathed in the warm glow of ships' lanterns, sample unique entrees such as Nasi Goreng, an Indonesian Sate of shrimp, beef or chicken, Boneless Quail roasted with Juniper berries, or an old German favorite, Hasenpfeffer braised in a red wine sauce. Stop by on Saturday and Sunday for lunch and brunch, so you can indulge in eye-openers like Beluga Caviar with iced Russian vodka or chilled champagne, Sea Lion Fizzes or a delicious Pink Dolphin. Delight in Glazed German Apple Pancake or for something a little more unusual, try Smoked Eel Frittata with Tomatoes and Chives. For dessert, Wolfgang and his crew have prepared delightful diversions in the form of Old English Trifle, light and creamy Rote Grutze, or rich slices of Black Forest Cherry Torte.

255

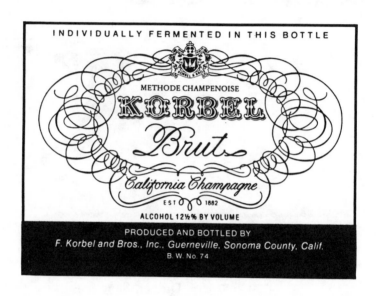

A medium dry champagne produced from the skillful blending of classic champagne grapes. The resultant cuvee is light, crisp and perfectly balanced.

Food Pairing: Glazed Ham or Duck a l'Orange and soup with a cream base, shellfish hors d'oeuvres and cakes.

Baked Clams

48 Cherrystone clams
1 oz. butter
¾ c. celery, diced ¼"
¾ c. onion, diced ¼"
¾ c. mushrooms, sliced
¼ c. parsley, chopped
½ t. thyme
1½ T. flour
2 T. sherry
¼ c. white wine
¾ c. cream
grated Parmesan cheese

Place clams in a pot, cover with water and boil for 10 minutes. Separate the clams from the shells. Save ¼ c. of the clam juice and 24 of the shells. Heat the butter in a separate saucepan and add the diced vegetables, parsley, thyme and clams. Saute for 1 minute and mix in the flour. Pour in the clam juice, sherry, white wine and cream. Bring to a boil and simmer for 2 minutes, stirring constantly. Remove from heat. Cover the bottom of 6 small casseroles with a thin layer of rock salt and place 4 shells in each. Fill the shells with the clam mixture and top with Parmesan cheese. Bake in a preheated oven at 450 degrees for 5 minutes or until golden brown on top.

Serves 6 as an appetizer

"Konigsberger Klosschen" Poached Meat Dumplings in Caper Sauce

Dumplings:

¼ c. onion, finely chopped
1 slice white bread, in fine crumbs
1 T. heavy cream
⅓ lb. ground pork
⅓ lb. ground veal
2 anchovy fillets, mashed
1 T. parsley, chopped
¼ t. salt
Pinch of white pepper
1 egg

Poaching liquid:

2 qts. water
1 medium onion, peeled and pierced with 6 whole cloves and
 2 bay leaves
2 T. salt
¼ T. white pepper

To prepare the meat dumplings thoroughly combine all ingredients and form into 1" balls. Refrigerate until ready to use. In a large pot bring all the poaching ingredients to a boil and drop in the dumplings. Simmer for 5 minutes and remove. Strain the liquid and set aside. Serve with Caper Sauce (recipe follows).

Serves 6

Caper Sauce

2 T. butter
2 T. flour
1½ c. stock from meat dumplings
1 T. capers
1 T. lemon juice
2 T. sour cream
1 egg yolk

In a heavy skillet melt the butter and mix with the flour. Add the stock while stirring constantly. Bring to a boil and simmer for 3 minutes. Add the capers and lemon juice, and simmer for another minute. Combine the sour cream and egg yolk and add to the sauce. Taste for seasoning and add the dumplings. Carefully simmer the sauce with the dumplings until hot. To serve, place 6-8 dumplings covered with sauce on each plate for an appetizer portion.

Yield: enough sauce for 6 appetizer portions

Zucchini and Ham Frittata

2 oz. clarified butter*
1 c. zucchini, washed and sliced
½ c. ham, diced
pinch of salt and pepper
¼ t. chopped basil
3 eggs

Heat 1 oz. of the butter in a skillet, add zucchini, ham, sprinkle of salt and pepper and the basil. Saute for 30 seconds and remove from heat. Beat the eggs in a separate bowl until well blended

Zucchini and Ham Frittata (con't)

and set aside. Heat the remaining butter in an omelette pan. Just before it begins to burn, add the eggs all at once. Add the zucchini and ham. With a wooden spoon move the mixture inward and shake the pan with the other hand. Continue this process until no egg liquid remains but they are still soft. Flip the frittata to brown and then return to its original position. To serve slide the frittata onto a warm place.

Serves 1

*See Glossary

Parisian Potatoes

4-5 lbs. potatoes (6-8 large Idahoes), peeled
3 c. water
¼ t. salt
4 T. clarified butter*
4 T. soft butter
2 T. parsley, finely minced

Scoop round little balls from the raw portions with a melon baller and drop into cold water to prevent discoloring. Put balls into a sauce pot, add the 3 c. water and the salt. Boil for 3 minutes. Drain them well and set aside. Heat the clarified butter in a large skillet, add potatoes and brown them, constantly shaking pan, over medium high heat. Remove any excess fat. To serve the potatoes add the softened butter and parsley and shake the pan until they are completely coated. Arrange on a heated platter and serve immediately.

Serves 6

*See Glossary

Hungarian Apple Strudel

Apple filling, marinated at least 24 hours (recipe follows)
6 sheets 10" x 14" filo dough
2 oz. melted butter
1 c. bread crumbs

On a clean, dry towel unfold 1 sheet of filo dough, the 14" side toward you, and brush it lightly with butter. Place another sheet along the upper edge of the first 1, overlapping it 1" and butter this lightly also. Sprinkle the breadcrumbs over the sheets and repeat 2 more times using 1 sheet each time, so you have 3 layers of filo, crumbs and butter. Line the apple filling in front of you on the top of the filo. Pull the towel under the filo over the filling away from you, rolling the apples into the filo. It should resemble a large sausage. Be sure the seam side is down. Pull the towel under the strudel away, brush with butter and sprinkle with breadcrumbs. Bake it in an oven set at 375 degrees for 40 minutes until golden brown. To serve the strudel cut at an angle, sprinkle with powdered sugar. Place each piece on warm plate and top with whipped cream.

Serves 6-8

Hungarian Apple Strudel Filling

5 apples, cored, peeled and cut into 10 sections
1 vanilla bean
4 oz. sugar
¼ c. lemon juice
¾ c. orange juice
2 sticks cinnamon
1 c. white wine
4 oz. raisins
2 oz. rum

Place prepared apples in a large saucepot. Split the vanilla bean in half, scrape out the seeds and add them with the pod to the apples. Add all remaining ingredients except the rum and bring to a boil. Remove the apples and simmer the juice until it becomes thick and syrupy. Return the apples to the liquid and add the rum, mixing gently. Refrigerate for 24 hours. Remove the vanilla bean and the cinnamon sticks before using.

Makes filling for 1 strudel

St. ORRES

36601 Highway 1 • Gualala, California 95445
(707) 884-3303

On a bright and beautiful rise overlooking a sandy cove, the St. Orres bids travelers seeking the exotic "welcome." Influenced by early Russian settlers the onion-domed mansion with stained glass windows exudes a magical quality. The Inn itself contains eight handcrafted rooms with intricate redwood-inlaid walls and soft velvet quilts. There are also nine fully equipped cottages arranged among the color-splashed gardens to provide views of the ocean, meadows and the musical St. Orres Creek, which are perfect for larger family groups, or executive meetings and seminars. An extravagant buffet breakfast is served each morning and in the evening savor a faultless and relaxing meal impeccably served under vaulted ceilings filled with natural light and soft greenery. Truly a memorable experience awaits at the St. Orres.

Terrine of Smoked Salmon

¾ c. fish veloute (fish stock thickened with 2 T. of roux*)
½ envelope gelatin, softened in ¼ c. water
¾ lb. smoked salmon
heavy cream, whipped to soft peaks (½ c. unwhipped)
3 T. chives, snipped

Heat veloute to boiling and add gelatin mixture to dissolve. Remove from heat and set aside. Process smoked salmon in a food processor fitted with a metal blade. Add veloute and gelatin mixture and process until smooth. Strain mixture by pushing through a coarse sieve. Fold in whipped cream and chives. Refrigerate for 15 minutes. Line a bread loaf pan with plastic wrap and fill with mousse. Cover top and refrigerate until set.

Garnish slice of terrine with sliced smoked salmon and golden caviar, if desired.

Serves 8

*See Glossary

Breast of Duckling with Honey

4 full breasts of duckling, skinned, boned and cut in half
  (reserve skins for cracklings)
salt and pepper to taste
flour
2 oz. peanut oil

Sprinkle duckling with salt and pepper, dredge in flour, shaking
off excess. Heat the peanut oil in a skillet over high heat. When
oil is hot, add duck breasts and saute for 2 minutes on each side
or until meat is just slightly pink inside. Keep duckling warm in
a low oven while making the sauce.

Cracklings:

Boil duck skins for 5 minutes, drain and place on baking sheet
in a medium oven until all fat is rendered and skins are crisp and
golden. Remove from oven, drain and lightly salt and pepper.
When cool, cut into ½" dice.

Sauce:

1 c. chicken stock, homemade or unsalted if canned
4 t. lemon juice
4 T. honey
huckleberries for garnish

Combine stock, lemon and honey in a saucepan and boil until
mixture is reduced by one third. Slice duckling on the diagonal,
allowing 1 whole breast per person. Sprinkle with cracklings
and huckleberries. Allow approximately ¼ c. of sauce per serving.

Serves 4

Pesto Angolotti with Garlic, Parmesan Cream and Sun-Dried Tomatoes

2 T. garlic, peeled and chopped
2 c. spinach, washed and chopped
½ c. mushrooms, sliced
3 T. sweet butter
2½ c. heavy cream
¼ c. sun-dried tomatoes, blanched to remove excess
  salt, chopped
¾ c. Parmesan, grated
1 lb. Pesto Angolotti, cooked
salt and pepper to taste
pine nuts to taste
basil or parsley to taste

Saute garlic, spinach and mushrooms in butter. Add cream and sun-dried tomatoes. Boil and reduce cream to desired consistency. Add ¼ c. of Parmesan, and the pasta. Heat to warm pasta and melt cheese. Season with salt and pepper. Garnish each plate with remaining cheese and pine nuts, basil or parsley (optional).

Serves 4

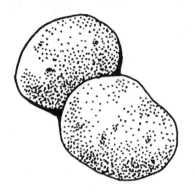

Custard Potatoes

1 T. sweet butter, melted
1½ t. garlic, peeled and chopped
3 large potatoes, peeled and sliced thin
1 pint heavy cream or half and half
4 eggs
salt and white pepper
pinch nutmeg
Parmesan cheese, grated

Rub the bottom of a 9" x 9" baking dish with melted butter and garlic. Arrange potatoes in dish.

Whisk heavy cream or half-and-half and eggs together. Season, oversalting to compensate for the potatoes. Pour mixture over potatoes in pan. Top with grated Parmesan cheese.

Bake at 350 degrees for 40 minutes or until potatoes are tender and custard is set.

Serves 8

Chilled Cantaloupe Soup

5 cantaloupes, peeled and seeded
½ c. apple juice
1 pint heavy cream
2 T. brandy or cassis

Blend cantaloupe and apple juice together. Strain into a container. Add heavy cream and brandy or cassis. Chill before serving.

Serves 10-12

Escargot Baked in Mushroom Caps

2 dozen escargot, simmered in white wine for 30 seconds
¼ c. pancetta*, cooked and chopped fine
2 dozen large mushroom caps

Drain escargot and set aside. Divide pancetta among mushroom caps. Top with escargot. Cover each escargot with escargot butter (recipe follows) and bake in oven-proof individual serving dishes at 500 degrees for 10 minutes or until mushrooms are cooked and butter is bubbling. Top each escargot with a toasted round crouton.

*See Glossary

Escargot Butter

Combine:

2 lbs. sweet butter
⅔ c. garlic, peeled and chopped
½ c. parsley, chopped
2 T. Dijon mustard
⅓ c. hazelnuts or almonds, blanched and chopped
   very fine
1 T. salt
2 t. white pepper
2 T. pancetta,* cooked and chopped fine
dash Worcestershire sauce

Combine all ingredients in a food processor.

Serves 6

*See Glossary

Blackberry Tart

Shortbread crust:

20 oz. all-purpose flour
7 oz. sugar
1 T. lemon peel, grated
1½ c. cold sweet butter, cut into small pieces
3 egg yolks

Combine flour, sugar and lemon peel. Cut in sweet butter until mixture resembles coarse meal. Add egg yolks and blend until dough holds together. Pat dough into 2 balls and chill. Roll out dough and fit into well-greased 10" tart pan(s) with removable bottoms. Prick bottom of shell(s) with fork and bake at 300 degrees for 30 minutes. Cool shell(s) before removing from pan.
This recipe makes 2 10" tart shells. You can make both shells at once and freeze one, or freeze half of the uncooked dough.

Almond Cream Filling

4 oz. cream cheese
½ c. powdered sugar
2 c. heavy cream
¼ t. almond extract
1 t. vanilla extract

Thoroughly cream together cream cheese, powdered sugar and a few tablespoons of the cream. Gradually add remaining cream and extracts, whipping to stiff peaks. Spread evenly into a cooled tart shell. Top tart with seasonal fruit, such as blackberries. Cut fruit used on tarts must always be glazed with a fruit glaze.
Yield: filling for 1 shell

35100 Highway 1 • Gualala, California 95445
(707) 884-3667

Celebrate life at the Whale Watch Inn, where the unparalleled Mendocino Coastline and an unhurried pace add up to an inspirational haven for local artists and visitors alike. The Inn is really a compound, comprised of five buildings containing eighteen individually decorated rooms and suites, on two acres overlooking Anchor Bay. Luxurious appointments, two-person spas and private decks present, in a brightly wrapped package, the magical beauty of the Anderson Valley and its dramatic ocean vistas. Arise refreshed and satisfy a sea-air sharpened appetite with a Continental-style breakfast of warm croissants, home baked nut breads, herbed cheese, eggs and fresh fruit compote. For those who seek the unusual, plan a visit during the annual whale migrations and see huge mammals gliding through azure seas, spewing white plumes into the air as they make their ancient pilgrimage to warmer waters.

271

Melted Brie with Almonds

1 wedge Brie cheese
2-3 T. butter, melted
¼ c. almonds, sliced and toasted (walnuts
    can be substituted)

Score a wedge of Brie cheese along surface. Pour the melted butter over Brie. Sprinkle with the toasted, sliced almonds (or chopped walnuts).

Heat on high in microwave, rotating at 7-second intervals, until partially melted. Serve with crackers.

Frittata

10 eggs
½ c. flour
1 t. baking powder
½ t. salt
1 pint small curd cottage cheese
1 lb. Jack cheese, shredded
½ c. butter, melted
8 oz. green chilies, diced

Beat eggs with mixer. Add flour, baking powder, salt and cottage cheese. Stir in Jack cheese, melted butter and chilies.

Grease 9" x 13" pan. Bake at 350 degrees for 35 minutes or until golden on top and knife comes out clean.

Mushroom Crust Quiche

5 T. butter
½ lb. mushrooms, chopped
½ c. saltine crackers, finely crushed
¾ c. green onions, chopped
2 c. Jack or Swiss cheese, shredded
1 c. cottage cheese
3 eggs
¼ t. cayenne pepper
¼ t. paprika

In frying pan over medium heat melt 3 T. butter; add mushrooms and cook until limp. Stir in crushed crackers. Turn mixture into well greased 9" pie pan. Press mixture evenly over bottom and sides.

In same frying pan over medium heat melt remaining 2 T. butter; add onions and cook until limp. Spread onions over mushroom crust. Sprinkle evenly with shredded cheese. In blender, whirl cottage cheese, eggs and cayenne pepper until smooth. Pour into crust and sprinkle with paprika.

Bake in 350 degree oven for 20-25 minutes or until knife inserted off-center comes out clean.

Let stand 10-15 minutes before cutting. *Freezes well*: Thaw, rewarm in 325 degree oven for 15 minutes.

Serves 4-6

MENDOCINO

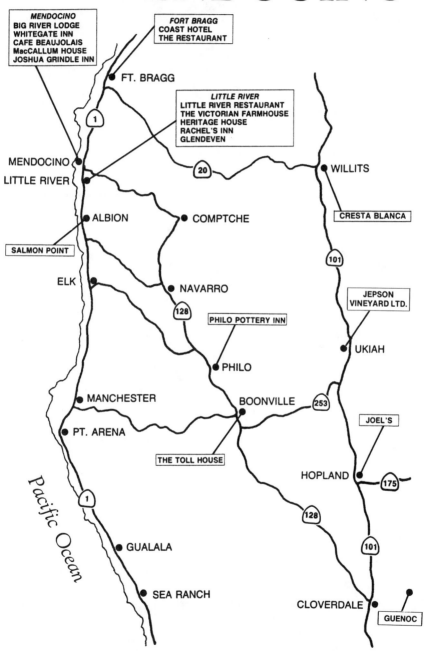

MENDOCINO
BIG RIVER LODGE
WHITEGATE INN
CAFE BEAUJOLAIS
MacCALLUM HOUSE
JOSHUA GRINDLE INN

FORT BRAGG
COAST HOTEL
THE RESTAURANT

FT. BRAGG

LITTLE RIVER
LITTLE RIVER RESTAURANT
THE VICTORIAN FARMHOUSE
HERITAGE HOUSE
RACHEL'S INN
GLENDEVEN

MENDOCINO
LITTLE RIVER

WILLITS

20

COMPTCHE

CRESTA BLANCA

ALBION

101

SALMON POINT

ELK

NAVARRO

JEPSON
VINEYARD LTD.

128

PHILO POTTERY INN

PHILO

UKIAH

MANCHESTER

BOONVILLE

253

JOEL'S

PT. ARENA

THE TOLL HOUSE

HOPLAND

175

Pacific Ocean

1

128

101

GUALALA

SEA RANCH

CLOVERDALE

GUENOC

RESTAURANT

3000 North Highway 1 • Albion, California 95410
(707) 937-0272
Hours: 5:00-10:00 p.m. Dinner, seven days a week
Credit Cards: Visa, M/C
Prices: Moderate
Reservations: Suggested
Specialties: Fresh game and fish

Alan Kantor and Josh Latkin are living proof that too many cooks don't necessarily spoil the broth. They work together creating marvelous food at the Salmon Point Restaurant. Ocean views, contemporary lines and a full, lively bar with dancing on Friday nights, make it a fun place to dine. A special innovative bill of fare, prepared in a gleaming kitchen, features entrees with fresh game and fish. Try a succulent Venison Stew, savor Rabbit with Oregon Truffles or fresh salmon in a preparation that varies nightly. If you are pressed for time call in your order and take it home. It is some of the best "fast" food.

277

Avocado Dressing

2 avocados
2 jalapeno peppers, seeded
1 clove garlic, chopped fine
1 lemon
1 lime
5 egg yolks
24 oz. peanut oil
4 oz. olive oil
4 oz. dry white wine
salt to taste

In food processor, puree avocados, jalapenos, garlic, juice of lemon and lime and the egg yolks. Slowly drizzle in both oils. Thin out dressing by drizzling in the wine. Salt to taste. Serve over your favorite green salad.

Yield: 1 quart

GARLIC

Artichokes Stuffed with Pork and Beef, with Crab Garnish

1 pint whole plum tomatoes
1 pint tomato puree
1 pint tomato sauce
¼ lb. hot Italian sausage, ground
¼ lb. beef, shredded
¼ lb. pork, shredded
6 cloves garlic, diced or minced
pinch fresh basil
pinch oregano
pinch granulated sugar
1 c. fresh Parmesan cheese
2 bay leaves
fresh ground pepper
2 oz. dry red wine
6 artichokes
1 c. fresh crab

Blend plum tomatoes and mix with tomato puree and tomato sauce. Brown sausage, beef and pork, and add to tomatoes. Saute garlic, add to sauce. Add fresh basil, oregano, sugar, ½ of the fresh Parmesan, bay leaves and fresh ground pepper. Stir, and add dry red wine to sauce. Simmer for 3 hours or longer. Strain meats from sauce and cool. Continue to simmer tomato sauce. Bring a pan of water to boil, and boil the artichokes; remove just before they are done. Cool, spreading the leaves. Stuff leaves with the meats and simmer the artichokes in the sauce for 5 minutes. Garnish with the remaining Parmesan cheese and fresh crab.

Serves 6

Scallop Mousse in
Lime Ginger Butter Sauce

12 oz. fresh New England sea scallops
2 eggs, separated
5 oz. heavy cream
pinch salt
pinch cayenne pepper
puff pastry
3 oz. fresh salmon fillet

Sauce:

thin slice of ginger root
6 oz. butter
4 oz. dry white wine
2 oz. heavy cream
juice from ½ lime
pinch salt
½ oz. brandy

Garnish:

pine nuts
chopped green onion

In food processor, puree scallops; keep machine running and drop in egg whites 1 at a time, reserving yolks. Drizzle in cream. (It is very important to keep machine running for good emulsification.) Add salt and cayenne pepper and put mixture in refrigerator until firm. Roll puff pastry to ⅛" thick and cut out 6 5" circles; refrigerate circles for 15 minutes. Make an egg wash by beating the egg yolks with 1 oz. of water. Lay out pastry circles and place scallop mixture in center of each circle, distributing mixture evenly.

Scallop Mousse in
Lime Ginger Butter Sauce (con't)

Place a strip of salmon on top of each. Brush the edges of each pastry circle with egg wash and fold pastry in half, enclosing the mousse. Crimp edges with fork. Brush egg wash across the top of each pastry, and bake at 350 degrees until golden brown, approximately 10-15 minutes.

Sauce: Slowly cook ginger slice in saute pan with ½ oz. of the butter for 1 minute. Add wine and reduce by half. Remove from heat, swirl in remaining butter; add cream, lime juice, salt and brandy. Stir until mixed and heated through. Immediately spoon sauce evenly on each plate. Place pastries on top of sauce. Garnish with pine nuts and green onions.

Serves 6

Grilled Chicken in Dijon
Mustard, Cream and Capers

6 boned chicken breasts
1 oz. butter
1 t. shallots, chopped
2 oz. dry white wine
12 oz. heavy cream
3 T. Dijon mustard
capers

Grill or barbecue chicken breasts. To make sauce, place butter in saute pan. Saute shallots until soft but not brown. Add wine and reduce until almost dry. Add cream and mustard, and reduce by half. Place sauce on plate, put chicken on top of sauce and sprinkle with capers.

Serves 6

Ginger Linguine Stir Fry
with Snow Peas, Red Bell Peppers
and Chicken

Pasta:

2 c. all-purpose flour
1 T. ginger root, grated
pinch of salt
3 eggs

Stir fry ingredients:

1 oz. peanut oil
½ oz. sesame oil
4 oz. snow peas
2 oz. red bell peppers, thinly sliced
6 oz. boned chicken, cut into ¼" dice
2 oz. cilantro, chopped
1 clove garlic, chopped fine
soy sauce to taste

Garnish:

green onion, chopped
almonds, sliced

Pasta: Place flour, ginger and salt in bowl. Add eggs to middle
of bowl and knead ingredients into a dough. Run dough through
pasta machine using the linguine cutter. Boil pasta until just done.
Stir fry: Heat peanut oil and sesame oil in either a large saute
pan or wok, over a high flame. When oil just begins to smoke
add snow peas, red bell peppers, chicken, cilantro and garlic. Cook
for 1 minute, stirring constantly. Add pasta and continue to cook
and stir. Add soy sauce and cook until chicken is cooked through.
Garnish with green onions and sliced almonds.

Serves 6

Petrale Sole Served with Chanterelles, Tomato and Tarragon

4 oz. milk
1 c. flour
6 Petrale sole fillets
1 oz. oil
4 oz. butter
6 oz. Chanterelle mushrooms
4 oz. cherry tomatoes, quartered
1 t. shallots, chopped
1 t. tarragon, chopped

Place milk in a bowl, and flour on a plate. Dip the fillets in the milk and then in the flour. In saute pan, place 1 oz. oil and 1 oz. of the butter. Heat until butter is melted and starts to bubble. Put fillets in pan and cook over high heat until brown; turn over and brown the other side.

Remove fillets from pan and place on plates. Drain excess oil from pan and add remaining butter, chanterelles, tomatoes, shallots and tarragon. Cook over high heat for 2 minutes. Spoon immediately over fish fillets.

Serves 6

Chocolate Hazelnut Ice Cream

10 oz. milk
5 oz. cream
5 oz. semisweet chocolate
4 oz. sugar
4 egg yolks
1½ oz. hazelnuts, roasted and chopped

In heavy gauge sauce pot, scald the milk and cream with the chocolate. Stir every once in a while to melt chocolate.

In a bowl whip together sugar and egg yolks.

When cream and chocolate mixture is scalded, temper the egg mixture by slowly drizzling in the cream mixture, whipping eggs vigorously. Put all ingredients in a double boiler and stir with rubber spatula until thickened slightly. Cool and freeze in an ice cream machine. Remove from machine and fold in hazelnuts.

Yield: 1 quart

LITTLE RIVER RESTAURANT

7750 North Highway 1 • Little River, California 95456
(707) 937-4945
Hours: 6:00 and 8:30 p.m., two seatings only for Dinner
Thursday through Sunday
Credit Cards: None
Prices: Moderate
Reservations: Recommended
Specialties: Good, straight-forward food

Inventive chef Jamie Griffith and his wife, Peggy, have created a silk purse out of a sow's ear with the converted gas station which houses the friendly Little River Restaurant. There are just seven tables in the low-ceilinged, candlelit dining room, so make reservations early and prepare to enjoy good, straight-forward cooking with a French influence and fresh California ingredients. Chef Jamie creates innovative entrees, such as his popular Quail with Hazelnut-Port Sauce, Pork Loin with Red Chili Currant Sauce or a tender Filet Mignon with Madeira Butter Sauce. Each entree comes with soup and salad du jour. Make reservations soon for a simply wonderful dinner. This one will become a favorite.

285

Caraway-Carrot Soup

1 medium yellow onion, chopped
1 c. water
1 lb. carrots, chopped fine
½ lb. yams, peeled and chopped fine
½ T. caraway seeds
4 cloves garlic, mashed and minced
1 pt. half-and-half
1 c. cream
1 T. raspberry vinegar
salt
white pepper

Place onions and water into pot; bring to a boil. Stir in carrots, yams and caraway. Cook until carrots are semi-tender. Stir in garlic; warm through. Puree carrot-yam mixture, and pour into double boiler. Add half-and-half and cream; warm through (about 30 minutes). Add vinegar; season with salt and white pepper to taste.

Serves 4

Poached Salmon Fillets

2 lbs. salmon bones, heads and tails
4 bay leaves
½ c. parsley, chopped
2 T. fennel seed
2 T. fresh thyme, chopped
salt
ground pepper
1½ lbs. yellow onions, chopped
1 T. fresh dill, chopped
4 6-oz. salmon fillets, cut on bias, ¾" thick

Place all ingredients, except salmon fillets, into a pot; bring to a boil. Reduce heat; simmer for half an hour. Strain mixture; adjust seasoning (it should be somewhat salty). Bring liquid back to a boil, and add the salmon fillets. Cook 2 minutes. Turn off heat, let steep until inner flesh of salmon is just opaque. Serve with Tarragon Cream (recipe follows).

Serves 4

Tarragon Cream
for Poached Salmon

½ c. fish stock (optional)
1 c. drinkable white wine
1½ T. fresh tarragon, chopped
3 shallots, minced
1 c. cream
salt
white pepper
lemon

Place stock, wine, tarragon and shallots into a pot. Reduce until

Tarragon Cream (con't)

almost evaporated. Add half of the cream. Season with salt and pepper to taste. Sauce should be slightly tart; add a squeeze of fresh lemon if necessary. If *too* tart, add a little more cream. Serve over poached salmon fillets.

Serves 4

Pecan Tart

Crust:

½ c. pecans, ground
1 c. flour
2 T. sugar
¼ t. salt
¾ stick unsalted butter
4 T. milk

Filling:

¼ c. brown sugar
2 eggs
⅔ c. light corn syrup
⅓ c. whipping cream
¼ c. rum
2 T. strong coffee
3 T. butter, melted
¼ t. salt
1½ c. pecans, coarsely chopped

Preheat oven to 325 degrees.
Crust: Blend pecans, flour, sugar and salt. Cut in butter. Add milk. Mixture should be moist. Roll out, and set into tart pan.
Filling: Whisk together brown sugar and eggs. Add corn syrup and cream; mix well. Add rum, coffee, butter and salt. Mix well. Lay chopped pecans in tart shell; pour filling over pecans. Bake about 35 minutes.

Serves 8

The Victorian Farmhouse

7001 Highway 1 • Little River, California 95456
(707) 937-0697

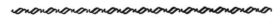

Cheery and warm are the adjectives that spring to mind at the mention of The Victorian Farmhouse. A quiet and soothing Bed and Breakfast Inn, just a pleasant walk from the ocean and two miles from the historic village of Mendocino, with its charming boutiques, galleries and gourmet restaurants. Stroll through the flower gardens or the apple orchard while listening to the bubbling music of the School House Creek. Four guest rooms with private baths have king or queen sized beds and are detailed with period antiques. A delightful breakfast is served "in room" each morning and complimentary sherry is served in the afternoon.

Cranberry Nut Loaf

2 c. flour
1½ t. baking powder
1 t. salt
½ t. baking soda
1 egg
1 c. sugar
¾ c. orange juice
3 T. vegetable oil
1½ c. cranberries, chopped
1 c. chopped nuts

Sift together flour, baking powder, salt and soda. In another bowl, blend until mixed egg, sugar, orange juice and oil. Stir in cranberries and nuts. Add dry ingredients and stir until barely moistened. Pour into a greased 9" x 5" x 3" loaf pan. Bake at 350 degrees for 45 minutes.

Serves 8

Applesauce Nut Bread

2 c. flour
¾ c. sugar
3 t. baking powder
½ t. baking soda
½ t. cinnamon
1 t. salt
1 egg, beaten
1 c. applesauce
2 T. shortening, melted
1 c. nuts, chopped

Mix first 6 ingredients together. Add egg, applesauce, melted shortening and nuts. Mix until blended. Pour into a greased loaf pan. Bake at 350 degrees for 1 hour.

Serves 8

Apple Kuchen

½ c. butter
½ c. sugar
2 eggs
½ t. vanilla or ½ t. grated lemon rind
1 c. cake flour
½ t. baking powder
½ t. salt
6 or 8 apples, sliced

Topping:

¼ c. butter
¼ c. flour
¼ t. cinnamon
1 c. sugar

Cream butter, sugar and eggs until creamy. Add vanilla or lemon rind, flour, baking powder and salt; spread in 2 greased coffee cake pans. Lay sliced apples on top of dough. Mix together topping ingredients, and sprinkle on top of the apples. Bake at 350 degrees about 25 minutes.

Serves 8

Zucchini Bread

2 c. sugar
½ t. cinnamon
1 t. baking soda
2 t. baking powder
¼ t. ginger
3 c. flour
¼ t. vanilla

Zucchini Bread (con't)

3 eggs, beaten
1 c. oil
½ c. nuts, chopped
2 c. zucchini, grated

Mix together the first six ingredients; add vanilla, eggs, oil, nuts and zucchini. Mix well. Bake in greased loaf pan at 350 degrees for 1 hour.

Serves 8

Sunday Morning Coffee Cake

¼ lb. butter
1 c. sugar
2 egg yolks
1 t. salt
2 t. baking powder
1¼ c. cake flour
½ c. milk
2 egg whites, beaten

Topping:

¼ c. sugar
½ t. cinnamon

In a large mixing bowl, cream butter, sugar and egg yolks. In another bowl add salt and baking powder to flour. Mix into butter and sugar mixture alternately with milk. Fold in beaten egg whites last. Pour into greased coffee cake pan. Mix together topping ingredients and sprinkle evenly on top of coffee cake. Bake at 350 degrees for 25-30 minutes.

Serves 6

Heritage House

5200 Highway 1 • Little River, California 95456
(707) 937-5885

The misty greens of the North Coast and the wind-hewn bluffs of Little River provide an ideal setting for the Heritage House. Built in 1887 by the Dennen family, the former smugglers' haven and gangster hideaway was fully restored in 1949 and transformed into a delightful Bed and Breakfast Inn surrounded by quaint, old-fashioned cottages. The Dennens' passion to preserve the history of their Inn is reflected in the Apple House. Originally located on a farm twenty-four miles away, it was dismantled and moved to the Inn where it has become a lounge with a full service bar. It's easy to appreciate your hosts' hospitality as you savor a glass of wine from the extensive, hand-picked wine list. A hearty breakfast and an enticing dinner in the ocean view dining room are included in the price of the room. Dinner features include innovative entrees, crisp, fresh vegetables and aromatic herbs, all grown on the abundantly flowered grounds.

Mushroom Clam Soup

4 c. clam juice
4 c. creme fraiche*
1 c. heavy cream
3 c. mushrooms, shredded
¼ c. lemon juice
2 T. garlic, chopped
salt and pepper to taste
3 c. whole baby clams

In a large stock pot heat the clam juice, creme fraiche, heavy cream and thicken the mixture with a roux*. Add the mushrooms, lemon juice, garlic, salt and pepper and simmer. One half hour before serving add clams and adjust seasonings.

Serves 12

*See Glossary

Port Wine Horseradish Glaze
(for Duck)

1 c. duck stock
4 T. currant jelly
1 T. horseradish
4 T. soy sauce
2 T. lime juice
¼ c. Ruby Port wine

Combine and heat all ingredients. Adjust flavors to taste. Thicken with cornstarch and cold water. Serve with roasted duckling.

Yield: 2 cups sauce

Red Pepper Raisin Relish
(for Lamb)

4 large red peppers
1 red onion, diced
2 green apples, peeled, cored and diced
¼ c. rice wine vinegar
⅓ c. water
¼ c. raisins
4 T. brown sugar
2 sticks cinnamon
1 T. curry powder
1 T. fresh ginger, minced
¼ t. ground cloves
1 T. tumeric
2 T. mustard seed
1 t. crushed red pepper flakes

Roast, peel and finely dice the red peppers. Saute onion and apple for 5 minutes, then add remaining ingredients and simmer until most of the liquid is gone. Place mixture in food processor and process using quick on-and-off pulses until it has the consistency of relish. Serve warm with roasted lamb.

Serves 6

Smoked Salmon Pasta

1 c. heavy cream
1 c. sour cream
2 c. smoked salmon, cut into thin strips
4 T. tomato paste
4 T. pesto*
1 sprig fresh rosemary
6 T. garlic chives, minced
3 T. garlic, chopped
3 T. lemon juice
2 T. lime zest, minced*
2 lbs. fresh pasta
1 c. freshly grated Parmesan cheese

Heat heavy cream and sour cream together in a large sauce pot and add all remaining ingredients except pasta and cheese. Simmer ½ hour. Cook pasta and ladle sauce over, sprinkle with cheese and serve.

Serves 4

*See Glossary

Apricot Pineapple Upsidedown Cake

Filling:

⅔ c. butter, melted
1½ c. brown sugar
1 fresh pineapple, peeled, cored and sliced ½" thick
1 c. dried apricots

Cake:

4 eggs, separated
¼ t. salt
1 c. sugar
2 t. grated citrus rind
1 t. lemon extract
1 c. flour
1 t. baking powder

Pour melted butter into stainless steel (so fruit won't discolor) 11" x 14" pan. Sprinkle in brown sugar and press lightly. Arrange pineapple slices and dried apricots in an attractive pattern over sugar. In a separate bowl beat egg whites with salt until stiff. Then beat in ½ c. sugar and set aside. In another bowl beat egg yolks with the remaining sugar, citrus rind and extract until thick, creamy, fluffy and light yellow in color. Pour over egg whites and fold lightly. Sift the flour and baking powder into mixture ⅓ at a time, folding gently. Be sure flour is completely blended. It will lose a little volume. Pour over fruit in pan and bake at 350 degrees for 30-40 minutes, or until a toothpick inserted in the center comes out clean. Let stand 15-20 minutes more before inverting onto serving plate. Best served warm with whipped cream.

Yield: 1 cake

MENDOCINO
CHARDONNAY

GROWN, PRODUCED AND BOTTLED BY JEPSON VINEYARDS LTD.
ALC. 13% BY VOLUME • UKIAH, CA • CONTAINS SULFITES

This elegant and complex Chardonnay is produced entirely from estate-grown grapes. The wine has a classic Chardonnay aroma of apples, lemons and just a hint of butterscotch. The taste is spicy and rich with a wonderful lingering aftertaste.

The ideal complement to all seafood, veal and poultry dishes.

Rachel's Inn

8200 North Highway 1 • Little River, California 95460
(707) 937-0088

Innkeeper Rachel Binah proudly acclaims "Comfort is my Business," and at Rachel's Inn she provides the perfect backdrop for harried guests to be nurtured and renewed. The recently renovated farmhouse has five rooms with private baths and a soft, soothing decor that reflects the concern Rachel has for her guests' every comfort. The walls of this quaint 1860's style Inn are enlivened with works of art created by Rachel and other local artists. Each night the rhythmic rise and fall of the surf will lull you to sleep and in the morning, awake to the smell of incredible homemade breakfast treats. After breakfast stroll through the multi-colored garden adjacent to a 160 acre park, where it is easy to witness the serene beauty of this charming Inn by the sea.

299

Mushroom Sauce

1 medium onion, chopped
6 T. butter
1½ lbs. mushrooms, sliced
3 T. flour
1 c. chicken stock
½ c. sherry
2 T. tamari
black pepper to taste
1 c. sour cream
¼ c. Parmesan cheese

Saute onion in butter. Add mushrooms and cook until liquid evaporates. Sprinkle flour over mushrooms, then add chicken stock, sherry, tamari and pepper; cook and stir. Add sour cream and Parmesan cheese.

If mixture is too thick, use chicken stock to thin; if too thin, continue cooking until sauce has reduced to desired consistency.

Serve with scrambled eggs. Usually prepared with 3 eggs per person, the mushroom sauce is spooned along 1 side of the eggs, and a border of finely sliced tops of green onion separates the yellow eggs from the brown sauce.

Yield: approximately 3 cups

Oatmeal Raisin Muffins

1 egg, slightly beaten
⅓ c. oil
1 c. buttermilk
1 t. vanilla
½ c. raisins
1¼ c. flour
2 t. baking powder
½ t. baking soda
1 t. salt
⅓ c. sugar
1 c. quick oats
1½ t. cinnamon
½ t. nutmeg

Beat egg with oil, buttermilk and vanilla. Add raisins and set aside.
In large bowl, sift flour with other dry ingredients. Mix well.
Add egg mixture to dry ingredients, combining gently. Do not overmix and do not beat.
Fill greased muffin tins ¾ full. Bake at 350 degrees for 30 minutes, beginning on the lower rack and finishing the last 10 minutes on the upper rack.

Yield: 10-12 muffins

Homemade Sausage

4 lbs. ground pork
8 cloves garlic, crushed
2½ T. leaf thyme
1 T. fennel seeds
½ t. crushed red pepper
⅛ t. black pepper
½ t. salt
¼ c. quick oats

Place pork in large bowl. Add garlic cloves to pork; sprinkle with remaining ingredients. Mix well with hands.

Form into patties and wrap individually with plastic wrap. Each patty can be compressed neatly by flattening after it is wrapped.

Freeze on a metal cookie sheet or a flat metal tray.

Baked Pears

6 pears, washed and cored
½ c. orange juice
1 c. brown sugar
cinnamon
nutmeg
butter

Place pears in buttered metal baking pan. Pour orange juice over pears. Put brown sugar in and around fruit. Sprinkle liberally with cinnamon and nutmeg. Place approximately 1 t. butter on each pear.

Bake at 350 degrees for 1 hour, or until pears are soft. Baste if fruit begins to brown on top.

If syrup is not thick when pears are done, remove pears to serving dishes and place pan on top of stove, boiling syrup to thicken. Spoon syrup over pears and serve.

Serves 6

Chocolate Marzipan Toasted Almond Torte

8 eggs, separated
1 c. butter
1 package (7 oz.) marzipan or almond paste
1 c. sugar
9 squares chocolate: 3 unsweetened, 6 semisweet,
   which have been melted and slightly cooled
2 c. toasted almonds, ground
¼ t. each vanilla and almond extract

Beat egg whites, refrigerate; set aside yolks. Cream butter and marzipan. Add sugar, beat until fluffy. Add (while beating) egg yolks, one at a time. Add slightly cooled chocolate, almonds and extracts. Gently fold in whipped egg whites. Bake at 350 degrees in greased springform pan. Ice with semisweet chocolate glaze.

Yield: 1 torte

Walnut (or Almond) Streusel Coffee Cake

Mix together in large bowl:
4½ c. unbleached white flour
1 t. salt
2 t. cinnamon
1 t. nutmeg
1 c. white sugar
2 c. brown sugar
1½ c. salad oil

Streusel topping:

Remove 1½ c. of above mixture to small bowl. Add to it:
2 c. walnuts, coarsely chopped (or sliced almonds)
1 T. cinnamon
1 T. nutmeg

Add to original mixture:
2 T. baking powder
2 T. baking soda
2 extra large eggs
2 c. buttermilk
2 T. vanilla

Beat until smooth. Pour batter into 2 springform pans which have been greased or sprayed with "Pam". Sprinkle streusel topping on cake and *gently* press into batter.
Bake at 350 degrees until a wooden toothpick comes out clean when inserted into the center of the cake, approximately 45 minutes.

Yield: 2 cakes

AKA "Little River Election Day Coffee Cake"

GLENDEVEN

8221 North Highway 1 • Little River, California 95456
(707) 937-0083

When planning a trip up the popular Mendocino Coast a "must stay" is the charming Bed and Breakfast Inn, Glendeven. The Maine-style farmhouse was originally built in 1867 and its companion, the Stevenscroft, named after Isaiah Stevens, builder of the main house, was added later. The delightful old country Inn has seven cozy rooms and the Stevenscroft has four, all with views of unfolding meadows and the Little River Bay. A mood of casual comfort with the accent on peace and quiet envelops the Glendeven. Each morning awake to a soft tapping on your door that means a generous breakfast has been delivered, or relax and enjoy the camaraderie of morning coffee in the comfortable sitting room.

305

Coffee Cake

2¼ c. flour
½ t. salt
1 t. cinnamon
¼ t. ginger
1 c. brown sugar
¾ c. white sugar
¾ c. salad oil
1 c. walnuts or pecans, chopped
1 t. cinnamon
1 t. baking soda
1 t. baking powder
1 egg
1 c. buttermilk

Heat oven to 350 degrees. Grease and flour a 9" x 13" x 2" pan. Mix together the flour, salt, 1 t. cinnamon, ginger, sugars and oil. Take out ¾ c. of this mixture, and add to that the nuts and the other teaspoon of cinnamon. Set aside (this is the topping).

To the remaining mixture, add baking soda, baking powder, egg and buttermilk. Mix until smooth. Spread in the pan. Sprinkle the topping on evenly and bake for 40-45 minutes.

Yield: 1 cake

Baked Apples

4 large, tart apples
¼ c. brown sugar
1 t. cinnamon
currants as desired
zest of ½ orange
butter

¾ c. boiling water
2 T. sugar *or*
¾ c. diluted frozen apple juice concentrate
whipped cream

Preheat oven to 375 degrees. Wash apples and remove core to ½" of bottoms. Combine the brown sugar, cinnamon and currants. Sprinkle orange zest over apples. Fill centers with sugar-cinnamon mixture. Dot with butter.

Place apples in 8" x 8" pan. Pour the boiling water mixed with the sugar *or* the apple juice around them.

Bake about 30 minutes until tender but not mushy. Baste occasionally with juices. Serve with whipped cream.

Serves 4

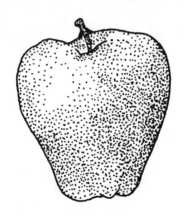

Highway 1 and Comptche-Ukiah Road
Mendocino, California 95460
(707) 937-5025

Discover Mendocino magic at the Big River Lodge. Embraced by magnificent forests and rugged coastal mountains on one side and the ever-changing Pacific on the other, the lodge provides superior accommodations with that friendly "at-home" feeling. The spacious rooms are thoughtfully decorated and the walls are adorned with local artists' works. Each room has its own bath, private entrance, woodburning stove and flower-lined deck with extraordinary views of the ocean and village of Mendocino. The landscaped grounds are also home to Big River Llamas, soft-eyed, good natured creatures which are highly prized for their wool. "Catch-a-Canoe" at the boat livery, swim in hidden pools and sun yourself on the white, sandy beaches along the Big River or explore the varied wildlife native to this enchanted area.

309

Hot Mulled Wine

1½ liters burgundy wine
1½ liters apple juice or cider
1 T. whole allspice
1½ t. cloves
2 broken cinnamon sticks
¼ t. Angostura bitters
4 T. Curacao
peel from 1 small orange, diced and soaked in the Curacao
sugar to taste

Mix all ingredients (including all of the orange peel and Curacao) in a large stainless steel saucepan or dutch oven. Heat to just below boiling. Mull for at least 20 minutes (longer is better). Strain if desired. Serve hot.

Yield: 3 liters

Holiday Shortbread

2 c. butter, softened
1¾ c. icing sugar, sifted
4½ c. white flour, sifted
food coloring (optional)

Cream butter, gradually beat in sugar. Add and beat in flour, a little at a time. Wrap dough in wax paper and chill. Pre-heat oven to 300 degrees. Allow dough to warm slightly; knead for 1 minute. Roll out dough on lightly-floured board to ¼" thickness, and cut with cookie cutters. Place cookies on ungreased cookie sheets. Decorate as desired (dough can be colored with food coloring for festive effect). Bake 15-20 minutes.

Note: if using Cuisinart, mix half of dough at one time.

Yield: 5 dozen cookies

Black Bottom Pie

1 c. sugar
2 T. cornstarch
4 c. scalded milk
4 egg yolks, beaten
2 t. vanilla
2 squares Baker's Chocolate
2 9" baked pie shells *or* graham cracker pie crusts
2 envelopes Knox Gelatin
½ c. water
2 t. rum flavoring or 2 T. rum
8 egg whites
1 c. sugar
2 c. whipped cream

Combine sugar and cornstarch. In another bowl, slowly add scalded milk to the egg yolks; stir in sugar mixture. Cook and stir in double boiler until custard coats spoon. Add vanilla. To 1 c. custard, add Baker's Chocolate (cut up). Stir until chocolate is melted. Pour into bottom of baked pie shell. Soften gelatin in water. Add to remaining hot custard. Stir until dissolved. Add rum flavoring or rum (be generous!). Cool until slightly thick. Beat egg whites, adding sugar gradually until stiff. Fold in custard-gelatin mixture. Pour over chocolate layer. Chill. Garnish with whipped cream.

Yield: two 9" pies

WHITEGATE INN
B E D & B R E A K F A S T

499 Howard Street • Mendocino, California 95460
(707) 937-4892

Innkeeper Patricia Patton welcomes guests "home" at the Whitegate Inn. Sheltered by ancient cypress trees and surrounded by a charming English garden enclosed by a white picket fence, the Inn exudes a warm feeling of comfort and well being. Patricia has decorated the old residence in a Victorian motif with an eye on its history and unique surroundings. Only six rooms, most with private bath, insure guests privacy and personal attention. An abundant breakfast of homemade everything—sweet breads, waffles, yogurt, special teas and blended coffee—is served each morning in the dining room. In the evening relax in front of a crackling fire while you sample some of Mendocino's finest vintages.

313

Whitegate Inn Waffles

1 c. white flour
⅓ c. whole wheat flour
2 t. baking powder
1 T. baking soda
1 T. cinnamon
4 eggs
1 T. sugar
1 c. buttermilk
¼ c. salad oil
2 T. vanilla
⅓ c. walnuts

Mix together flours, baking powder, baking soda and cinnamon. Beat eggs thoroughly. Mix in sugar, add buttermilk, oil and vanilla and mix well. Combine flour mixture and egg mixture and mix lightly. Add walnuts.
Cook as directed for waffle iron.
Note: Diced apples may also be added to batter or sliced bananas may be placed on top of batter before closing waffle iron lid. If batter appears too thick, additional buttermilk may be added.

Serves 4

Strawberry Butter

1 lb. butter
½ c. strawberries (fresh or frozen)
¾-⅔ c. powdered sugar

Combine all ingredients in food processor until completely blended.

Apricot Butter

1 egg
½ c. powdered sugar
2 lbs. butter
1 lb. ground dried apricots (to grind, freeze apricots
  and then grind in food processor)
1½ c. walnuts, ground

In food processor beat egg, add sugar and blend completely. Add butter and mix thoroughly, scraping sides occasionally with spatula. Add apricots, blend well; add walnuts and process until blended.
Both butters are best stored frozen.

Pineapple Carrot Bread

3 eggs
2 c. sugar
1 c. oil
3 T. vanilla
2 c. grated carrots
2 c. white flour
1 c. whole wheat flour
1 t. baking powder
1 t. baking soda
1 t. salt
1 8-oz. can crushed pineapple, slightly drained
1 c. nuts, chopped
½ c. raisins (optional)

Preheat oven to 350 degrees. Grease 2 9" x 5" pans. Beat eggs; add sugar, oil, vanilla and blend well. Add carrots. Sift together flours, baking powder, baking soda and salt, and add to egg mixture. Blend well. Stir in pineapple, nuts and raisins; mix well. Bake 1 hour and cool in pans.

Yield: 2 loaves

Patricia's Granola

½ c. salted, roasted sunflower seeds
5 c. oatmeal
⅓ c. oil
⅓ c. honey
¼ c. brown sugar
1 t. vanilla
1 pinch cinnamon (more if desired)

Combine the above ingredients, stirring until completely blended (this may take 5 minutes or so but is the secret to good granola). Spread mixture on jellyroll pan and bake at 350 degrees for 30 minutes or until golden, stirring frequently.

Cool and add:
½ c. toasted almonds
¼ c. toasted salted almonds, diced
½ c. raisins
¼ c. shaved toasted coconut
and/or:
½ c. dried apricots, diced
½ c. dried apples, diced
½ c. walnuts, diced

CAFE BEAUJOLAIS

961 E. Ukiah Street • Mendocino, California 95460
(707) 964-0292
Hours: 8:00 a.m.-2:30 p.m., Breakfast seven days a week
11:30 a.m.-2:30 p.m., Lunch seven days a week
6:30-9:30 p.m., Dinner Wed. through Sun. May through Oct.
Credit Cards: Cash only
Prices: Moderate
Reservations: Suggested
Specialties: International Favorites with a California Flair
and Scrumptious Desserts

Margaret Fox's all-consuming passion is food and to experience the fruits of her labor first hand is worth a trip to lovely Mendocino and the Cafe Beaujolais. In a Victorian house near the center of town Margaret works her magic. The homey touches, flowered wallpaper, shiny hardwood floors, antique chairs and fresh flowers on the tables build a mood of anticipation that climaxes in pure eating enjoyment. A menu of carefully selected favorites with a California flair pleases not only the palate but the eye as well. Margaret doesn't stop with a successful restaurant. She has become famous for her Panaforte Di Mendocino (rich Italian fruitcake) which has been critically acclaimed and shipped to finer stores across the country. And if that isn't enough she has written a cookbook that reveals her genius and some of her secrets, too.

317

Walnut Vinaigrette and Salad

1 c. toasted walnut halves
½ c. walnut oil
2 T. lemon juice, strained
½ t. salt
a few grinds of black pepper
¼ t. Dijon mustard (optional)
butter lettuce for 4, or a mixture of lettuce, watercress
and chopped Belgian endive; washed, dried, crisp and cold

Toast walnuts for 10 minutes in a 350 degree oven. Rub skins off by tossing in a strainer. Combine oil, lemon juice, salt and pepper and optional mustard. Place greens and walnuts in bowl. Toss with dressing.
Serve on chilled plates.

Serves 4

Zucchini-Curry Soup

4 zucchini, cut into thick slices
1 onion, chopped
1 T. curry powder (excellent quality)
3 c. chicken stock
salt
pepper
¾ c. half-and-half
½ c. whipped creme fraiche*
½ c. chives, chopped
chive blossoms (if available)

Place zucchini, onion, curry powder and chicken stock in a saucepan. Cover and simmer for 25 minutes. Stir occasionally. Puree mixture in a blender, strain, add salt and pepper to taste and half-and-half.
Serve in heated bowls with a dollop of whipped creme fraiche, a sprinkling of chopped chives and, if possible, a chive blossom per bowl.

*See Glossary

Serves 5-6

Pollo Del Sol

1 chicken, cut into 8 serving pieces
3 T. olive oil
4 cloves garlic, minced
1 onion, finely chopped
¾ c. dry white wine
1 small lemon, thinly sliced, seeds removed
12 Italian dried olives
4 sun-dried or oven-dried tomatoes, slivered

Step 1. Prepare the chicken pieces
Blot chicken pieces with paper towels until they are dry. Heat olive oil in a large skillet. When the oil is very hot, but not smoking, saute the pieces of chicken skin side down. Saute for 10 minutes on one side, then 5 minutes on the other side. Remove chicken from skillet, and set aside.

Using the same oil in the skillet, cook the garlic and onions over medium heat for 5 minutes, or until the onions are tender. Over high heat, add the wine and all chicken parts except the breast. Add salt and pepper to taste, cover, and simmer for 15 minutes. After 15 minutes, turn chicken pieces over and add breasts, lemon slices, tomatoes and olives.

Cover and cook 15 minutes more. Remove chicken from skillet, arrange on platter.

Step 3. Prepare sauce and serve
Turn up heat, and quickly reduce the liquid until it starts to become syrupy. Spoon it and the tomatoes, lemon and olives over the chicken pieces, and serve.

Serves 4

Armenian Rice Pilaf

8 oz. unsalted butter, cut into tablespoon-size pieces
4 c. chicken stock
freshly ground black pepper
1½ t. salt
3 T. safflower or other light oil
1⅓ c. loosely packed vermicelli broken into
    1 to 1½" pieces
2 c. long grain white rice
½ c. toasted pine nuts or blanched unsalted almonds
    (optional)

Put butter and chicken stock into a 2-quart saucepan. Add 5 or 6 grinds of black pepper and the salt. Bring to a boil. If boiling occurs before next step is completed, cover and reduce heat. It must be boiled again before proceeding.

In a heavy-bottomed 3-to-4 quart casserole, heat the oil until hot. Add vermicelli, stirring rapidly and constantly until light gold in color. Add the rice, stirring constantly. Continue to stir the mixture until most of the rice grains have turned from dull white to slightly translucent, with a bright white center. The vermicelli should be uniformly golden. This entire process should take 5 or 6 minutes if the heat is right.

Remove from heat. Very slowly, with your face well away from the casserole, pour the boiling stock/butter mixture over the rice/vermicelli mixture. Return to stove and adjust the heat to the lowest possible setting. Cover tightly and let simmer for 25 minutes.

Slide cover slightly off the casserole and let cook for 10 more minutes. Do not stir the rice or the pilaf will become mushy and broken. Look at the pilaf. The vermicelli should be beginning to curl. Let rest for 15 more minutes. Correct seasoning if necessary. If you wish, gently fold in toasted pine nuts or blanched unsalted almonds.

Serves 8

Lemon Ice Cream

5 T. lemon juice, strained
grated rind of 2 lemons
¾ c. white sugar
2 c. heavy cream
1 pinch salt
⅛ t. nutmeg
more nutmeg, toasted walnuts, fresh mint (optional)

Stir together all ingredients, making sure sugar is dissolved. Pour into an 8" square pan and place in your freezer. (You can also strain it before freezing, if you'd prefer a perfectly smooth texture.) Every 30 minutes, stir, taking care to scrape the outside frozen parts into the middle. It will be ready in about 3 hours.

Optionally, top with nutmeg or toasted walnuts, and serve with a sprig of mint.

Serves 4

MacCALLUM HOUSE
RESTAURANT

4520 Albion St. • Mendocino, California 95460
(707) 937-0289
Hours: 6:00-10:00 p.m. seven nights a week
Credit Cards: None, but personal checks are accepted.
Prices: Moderate to expensive
Reservations: Required on weekends
Specialties: New American Seasonal & Regional

Feast seven nights a week on New American and Regional cuisine at the MacCallum House. The old Victorian home has been recently updated, but remains true to its heritage. The European-style dining room is enhanced with dark walnut wainscoting, Victorian print wallpaper, curtains of European lace and a cheery, native rock fireplace. The restaurant's charming bar, The Grey Whale, is in an enclosed sunporch filled with macrame window hangings and lots of plants. The chef at the MacCallum House uses the freshest possible ingredients to create succulent dishes like melt-in-your-mouth Stuffed Mushrooms, a beautifully presented Seafood Pate in Basil Sauce, Broiled Veal Chops with Walnut and Roquefort Butter or Duck Confit with Chanterelles and Lingonberries. For a memorable dining experience make your next dinner reservations at the MacCallum House.

323

Indian Split Pea and Vegetable Soup

2 qts. chicken stock
½ lb. split peas
½ t. cumin
½ t. coriander
½ t. turmeric
½ t. black pepper
½ t. salt
6 oz. butter
1 large yellow onion, diced
1 carrot, diced
1 stalk celery, diced
1 eggplant, peeled, diced
1 yellow squash, diced
1 t. garlic, minced
1 t. ginger, minced
1 c. cream
1 bunch spinach leaves, chopped
juice of 1 lime
almonds, sliced

In a heavy pot bring the stock to a boil. Add the split peas and all the spices. Keep at a simmer and stir occasionally.
In a large saute pan melt the butter and cook the diced vegetables, garlic and ginger. When the onions are translucent, add the vegetable mixture to the peas. Cook until the peas are done. Add the cream, spinach leaves and the lime juice. Garnish with almonds.

Serves 4-6

Seafood Pate in Basil Sauce

6 oz. salmon
1 egg
7 oz. cream
salt and pepper
14 oz. cod, pureed (or equal amounts of trout and shrimp)
3 eggs
28 oz. cream
¼ c. fresh parsley
salt and pepper
2 oz. each salmon, cod and shrimp, diced

Basil Sauce:
½ onion, diced
1 t. garlic
1 t. basil
1 t. olive oil
24 oz. tomato juice
2 T. fresh parsley, chopped
salt and pepper to taste

Place the food processor bowl in refrigerator for ½ hour before ready to use.

Process salmon, egg, cream, salt and pepper. Refrigerate 1 hour. Puree cod. Then add eggs, cream, parsley, salt and pepper. Add diced fish to the pureed cod mixture. Butter a terrine. Pour half the cod mixture into the terrine. Add the salmon mousse. Cover with the cod mixture. Cover the terrine with wax paper and tin foil. Bake 1 hour at 375 degrees.

Basil Sauce:
Saute onion, garlic and basil in olive oil. Add tomato juice and simmer 15 minutes. Add parsley and adjust seasoning.

Place basil sauce on the plate. Add slice of seafood pate on top of the sauce.

Serves 6 as an appetizer

325

ESTATE BOTTLED
MENDOCINO
ZINFANDEL

PRODUCED AND BOTTLED BY CRESTA BLANCA VINEYARDS
UKIAH, MENDOCINO COUNTY, CALIFORNIA
ALCOHOL 12% BY VOLUME

A full bodied red with the unique raspberry character,
fruity taste and a hint of oak flavors.

Wonderful with lamb, veal, stews, duck in flavorful sauces,
stronger cheeses and especially chocolate.

Broiled Veal Chops with Walnut and Roquefort Butter

½ c. red wine
1 T. shallots, sliced
pinch of thyme
¼ c. soft butter
2 t. walnuts, finely chopped
T. parsley, chopped
1½ T. Roquefort cheese
salt and pepper to taste
2 7 oz. veal chops

Reduce wine, shallots and thyme by ½. Stir in butter, walnuts, parsley and cheese. Refrigerate.
Salt and pepper the veal chops. Broil to desired doneness. Top with the Roquefort butter and serve.

Serves 2

Duck Confit with Chanterelles and Lingonberries

1 large duck
salt and pepper
1 T. garlic, minced
1 bay leaf
2 oz. vegetable oil
1 large onion, chopped
1 large carrot, chopped
2 stalks celery, chopped
1 head garlic, chopped

Duck Confit (con't)

1 tomato, chopped
2 oz. chanterelle mushrooms
¼ c. whipping cream
1 oz. lingonberries

Remove both breasts, the legs and thighs from the duck. Rub salt, pepper, garlic and bay leaf on the breast and dark meat. Cover with plastic wrap and refrigerate overnight.
Remove all fat and skin from the duck carcass. Cut fat in small pieces and put it in a pot. Place on low heat and melt the fat. (It will take at least an hour.) Strain the fat. Throw away the solids. Make a duck stock by chopping the duck bones and browning them in a 400 degree oven. Put the browned bones in a large pot and cover with water. Bring to a boil and reduce to a simmer. Brown the vegetables in the oil and add to the bones. Cook 4 hours. Strain. Reduce the liquid to about a cup.
The next day wipe the spices off the duck meat. Place in a baking dish and cover with the rendered duck fat. Bake in a 325 degree oven for 1½ hours.
To assemble: heat the duck stock. Add the chanterelles, the cream and the lingonberries. Taste for salt and pepper. Take the duck meat out of the fat and wipe with paper towels. Add the meat to the sauce and serve.

Note: You have to start this dish 1 day before you plan on serving it.

Serves 2

Stuffed Mushrooms

12 oz. cream cheese
5 oz. sour cream
1 chicken bouillon cube
1 t. lemon juice
1 t. garlic
1 t. butter
½ t. Worcestershire sauce
4 oz. mushrooms, chopped
1 T. flour
1 T. melted butter
24 large button mushroom caps

In a heavy sauce pan melt the cream cheese, sour cream, bouillon cube and lemon juice. Saute the garlic in butter and add to the cream cheese mixture. Add Worcestershire sauce and chopped mushrooms. Make a roux* by stirring the flour into the melted butter and add that to the cream cheese mixture. Cook mushroom caps in microwave or the oven until tender. Pour cream cheese mixture into a pastry bag and pipe into the mushroom caps. Bake in 350 degree oven until lightly browned.

Serves 6 as an appetizer

*See Glossary

JOSHUA GRINDLE INN

44800 Little Lake • Mendocino, California 95460
(707) 937-4143

Innkeepers Gwen and Bill Jacobson invite their guests to sample a serene, home-away-from-home atmosphere far from the pressures of demanding schedules. Originally built in 1879 by its namesake, The Joshua Grindle Inn is located in the historic village of Mendocino and offers charming views of the bay and ocean. The rooms have private baths with views of surrounding countryside and ocean vistas, each filled with country antiques from the innkeepers' own collection. It's easy to leave your car keys in the room because the Art Center, galleries, quaint shops, excellent restaurants and rugged Mendocino Coast are all a pleasant stroll away.

331

Buttermilk Muffins

2 c. flour
  (could substitute ¼ c. whole wheat flour for variety)
½ c. sugar
1 T. baking powder
¾ t. salt
½ t. baking powder
1 egg, slightly beaten
1 c. buttermilk
¼ c. (½ stick) melted butter or margarine

Preheat oven to 400 degrees. Mix together the first 5 ingredients then add the next 3. Stir until dry particles are moistened. Fill muffin cups about ⅔ full. Bake for 15 minutes, or until done when tested.

This is a basic recipe. For *Pumpkin Muffins* add:

½ small can pumpkin
½ t. cinnamon
¼ t. ginger
⅛ t. ground cloves

Basic recipe plus blueberries, apple, pineapple, etc., etc. Lots of possibilities.

Yield: 12 muffins

Strawberry Muffins

4½ c. flour
1¼ c. sugar
2¼ T. baking powder
1⅔ t. salt
1¼ t. baking soda
1 pt. strawberries, chopped
3 eggs, slightly beaten
1 t. almond extract
2¼ c. buttermilk
1 stick (¼ lb.) margarine, melted
cinnamon/sugar mixture for topping

Combine flour, sugar, baking powder, salt and baking soda. Add chopped strawberries. Mix. Add eggs, almond extract, buttermilk and margarine. Mix until dry ingredients are moistened. Fill greased muffin cups ⅔ full. Top with cinnamon/sugar mixture. Bake 15 minutes or until done in a 375 degree oven.

Yield: 36 muffins

Crustless Quiche

½ c. butter
12 eggs
½ c. flour (Wondra)
1 t. baking powder
½ c. butter, melted
1 8 oz. can green chilies (Ortega diced—7 oz.)
1 pt. cottage cheese
1 lb. Jack cheese, grated

Grease 13" x 9" x 2" pan. Beat eggs lightly and add flour, baking powder. Blend and add melted butter, diced chilies, cottage cheese and Jack cheese. Mix until just blended, pour into pan. Bake at 400 degrees for 15 minutes, then 350 degrees for 35-40 minutes. Check to make sure it is baked clear through.

Applesauce Muffins

4½ c. flour
1¼ c. sugar
4½ t. baking powder
2¼ t. salt
1¼ t. soda
1 t. allspice
1 jar (25 oz.) applesauce or 2 c. homemade applesauce
½ c. white raisins
3 eggs
¾ c. milk
¾ c. oil

Combine flour, sugar, baking powder, salt, soda and allspice in a large bowl. In another bowl combine applesauce, raisins, eggs, milk and oil. Let sit long enough for raisins to soften. (Wet ingredients may sit, covered, overnight in the refrigerator.) Add wet ingredients to dry and mix until dry ingredients are moistened. Fill greased muffin cups ⅔ full. Bake 15 minutes or until done in a 375 degree oven.

Yield: 34-36 muffins

101 N. Franklin • Fort Bragg, California 95437
(707) 964-6443
Hours: 11:00 a.m.-3:00 p.m. Lunch, Tues.-Sat.
5:00-9:00 p.m. Dinner, Thursday.
6:00-10:00 p.m. Dinner, Fri. and Sat.
Credit Cards: Am. Express, Visa, M/C
Prices: Moderate
Reservations: Suggested for dinner
Specialties: Creole Cooking

Hidden in the old Coast Hotel in Fort Bragg is a little gem of a restaurant, appropriately named the Coast Hotel Cafe. The restaurant is an unpretentious little cafe with a low parquet ceiling and lots of brass accents. It serves delectable creole cooking with a California flair. Spicy Black Roux Gumbo, Jambalaya and Shrimp Creole are just a few of the exciting entrees, and for those with milder tastes there is Oysters Bienville, Steak and Onions or Pork Chops Louisiana style. Also in the hotel is Carol Halls' Hot Pepper Jelly Co., which features hot pepper jellies, herbs, vinegars, mustards and a lot more exciting homemade condiments, some of which are served alongside the tasty entrees from the Coast Hotel Cafe.

Oysters Bienville

¼ c. butter
3 T. flour
1 clove garlic, minced
1 T. onion, grated
1 T. Worcestershire sauce
½ lb. mushrooms, slivered
¾ c. liquid (shrimp or mushroom stock)
1 dozen raw shrimp, chopped
1 T. white wine
2 dozen oysters on the half shell
Parmesan cheese, freshly grated

In the top of a double boiler, combine butter and flour. Stir until smooth. Add next 7 ingredients and cook until sauce becomes smooth and medium thick. Spoon sauce on each oyster and place under broiler for 2 minutes. Remove from oven, sprinkle with Parmesan cheese and broil 2 more minutes. Serve hot and enjoy.

Serves 4 as entree or 8 as appetizer

Coast Straight Chili

1 qt. beef stock
2 lbs. ground beef
1½ c. onions, chopped
5 T chili powder
1 t. ground cinnamon
1½ t. ground cumin
¼ t. ground cloves
¼ t. cayene pepper
1 15 oz. can tomato sauce
2 T. vinegar
½ square unsweetened chocolate

Boil stock and add meat in small pieces. Cover and simmer for

Coast Straight Chili (con't)

about 20-30 minutes. Add remaining ingredients. Bring to a boil, reduce heat and simmer for 1 hour stirring occasionally. Refrigerate overnight. Skim fat before re-heating and serving.

Serves 6

Sausage Jambalaya

½ lb. andouille sausage
½ lb. ground "country style" sausage
½ lb. ham
½ lb. smoked sausage
2-3 medium to large onions, medium chopped
1 large green bell pepper, medium chopped
3 cloves garlic, minced
1 large can whole tomatoes
Louisiana hot sauce, to taste
2 c. raw rice
2-3 c. water

Cut all meats (any combination of the above or chicken will do just fine(into bite size pieces. Place first 7 ingredients in a heavy dutch oven and saute until vegetables are limp. Add tomatoes and hot sauce. Simmer all ingredients for about 20 minutes. Add raw rice and water (enough liquid is needed to cook the rice). Bring mixture to a boil, cover, turn to lowest heat and cook until rice is done. Serve hot. Accompany the jambalaya with a tossed salad and fresh fruit for a complete meal.

Serves 6

Queen Ida's Pecan Pie

3 eggs
1 c. sugar
1 c. white Karo syrup
1 c. pecans, chopped
1 t. pure vanilla
pinch of salt
1 9" pie shell, unbaked

Beat eggs. Add sugar and remaining ingredients. Mix well. Pour into unbaked pie shell and bake at 325 degrees for 1 hour.

Serves 6-8

The Restaurant

∽∾∽∾∽∾∽∾∽∾∽∾∽∾∽∾∽∾∽∾∽

418 Main St. • Fort Bragg, California 95437
(707) 964-9800
Hours: **11:30 a.m.-2:00 p.m. Lunch, Mon., Tues., Thurs. and Fri.**
5:00-9:00 p.m. Dinner, every night except Wed.
10:00 a.m.-1:00 p.m. Brunch, Sunday
Closed all major holidays and the month of March
Credit Cards: M/C and Visa
Prices: Moderate
Reservations: Recommended
Specialties: "Anything they want"

∽∾∽∾∽∾∽∾∽∾∽∾∽∾∽∾∽∾∽∾∽

If you like to "discover" places, and casual cafe dining is up your alley, across from the Skunk Railroad Station is the landmark building which houses The Restaurant. It was originally designed in 1895 to serve as the first hospital. Jim Larsen and his wife, Barbara, together with partner Rose Nunes, have developed a no-nonsense approach to food and disdain food snobs who breeze in and say, "Show me what you can do!" They can do plenty! Snacking on spicy Anchovy Spread with crusty French bread whets the appetite while paintings and sculptures amuse the eye. For dinner succumb to Jim's own version of Blackened Redfish (he uses salmon) or perhaps sample Shrimp with Tomatoes, Cream and Shallots. Finish with a fresh fruit tartlet or a slice of ultra-creamy cheesecake and steaming cups of coffee. Even the bill will make you smile.

339

Scallops with Aquavit and Creme Fraiche

2 lbs. bay scallops
6 T. Aquavit**
2 t. grated lemon zest
¼ c. fresh dill, chopped
¼ t. salt
1½ c. creme fraiche*
¼ c. Dijon mustard
paprika

In a large bowl mix scallops with Aquavit, lemon zest, dill and salt. Divide evenly between 8 small casseroles. Mix creme fraiche* with mustard and spoon over each casserole. Sprinkle sparingly with paprika. Chill, covered, for 3 hours or more. Preheat broiler. Broil 6" from heat until tops are browned and scallops are just cooked, 4-5 minutes. Serve immediately.

Serves 8

*See Glossary
**Clear Scandinavian liquor flavored with caraway.

Grilled Polenta with Prosciutto and Fontina

6 c. water
1 t. salt
2 c. polenta*
½ c. butter
½-1 c. grated Parmesan cheese
8-10 thin slices prosciutto ham
8-10 thin slices Italian Fontina cheese
fresh sage leaves

In large deep pot over full heat, bring water and salt to a boil; slowly stir in the polenta*. Reduce heat and simmer gently, stirring frequently until very thick (15 to 20 minutes). Add butter and Parmesan cheese, stir until smooth. Pour into well-buttered 9" x 5" loaf pan. Smooth top. Cover and chill for several hours. When cold, unmold and slice in 8 to 10 slices. Grill each slice in butter on 1 side until golden brown; turn over, put a slice of prosciutto and a slice of Fontina on top; cover for 2 or 3 minutes until cheese has melted. Serve as a first course. Garnish with some fresh sage leaves.

Serves 8-10

*Italian cornmeal

Creme Brulee

2 c. heavy cream
1 t. vanilla
5 egg yolks
½ c. plus 1 T. granulated sugar
pinch of salt
¼ c. plus 1 T. brown sugar

Preheat oven to 325 degrees. In heavy sauce pan, heat cream over moderate heat until hot but not scalded; add vanilla. In large mixing bowl, beat egg yolks and sugar until mixture is thick and pale. Add salt, mix until combined and beat in cream mixture thoroughly. Divide mixture between 7 or 8 ¾ c. ramekins. Set ramekins in baking pan large enough to accommodate them without touching. Add enough hot water to reach halfway up sides of ramekins. Bake in preheated oven until knife inserted in center comes out reasonably clean or until you can see that custard is quite thick. Remove ramekins from pan and cool on rack. Turn on broiler. Place custards on baking sheet. Force brown sugar through sieve over custards. Watching very carefully, broil 1 to 3 minutes, just until sugar has melted or carmelized. Remove; chill for 6 hours or overnight.

Serves 7 or 8

13500 So. Highway 1 • Hopland, California 95449
(707) 744-1328
Hours: 11:30 a.m.-2:30 p.m., Lunch
5:30-9:30 p.m., Dinner
10:00 a.m.-2:30 p.m. Sunday Brunch
Closed Monday and Tuesday
Credit Cards: All Major
Prices: Moderate
Reservations: Suggested
Specialties: California Fresh

Joel and Nancy Clark together with Chef Peter O'Carroll have created a warm, family restaurant that has become a favorite of local residents, and rightfully so. Chef O'Carroll's love of good food shines in his presentation, intriguing daily specials and generous portions for hearty appetites. Savory entrees like Beef Wellington with homemade pate, grilled steaks and chicken or piquant veal sautes and spicy rabbit sausages headline a menu designed to please local and visiting palates and showcase the wonderful fresh meats and vegetables available in the area.

343

Prawns and Prosciutto Over Pasta

8 oz. clarified butter*
1-1½ lbs. large cleaned peeled prawns
¼ lb. thinly sliced prosciutto strips
1 large yellow onion, chopped
1 T. minced garlic (about 3 cloves)
1 T. dried tarragon
pinch each of salt, pepper and granulated garlic
2 c. white wine
16 oz. (1 lb.) of fresh fettuccine
 or 8 oz. of dried fettuccine
⅛ lb. (2 oz.) Parmesan cheese, grated
1 lemon, cut into wedges
parsley

Using a high flame, heat 4 oz. butter in large saute or frying pan. When hot add prawns, prosciutto, onion, garlic, green onions, tarragon, parsley, salt, pepper and granulated garlic. Let this saute over high heat to lightly brown prawns and soften other ingredients. Reduce flame to ⅓ and add wine. Stir ingredients around pan, add remaining butter and increase flame to ½. Let simmer and reduce. Let pasta cook or reheat dried cooked pasta. Drain pasta and place equally on plates. Arrange prawns over pasta, pour remaining liquid and ingredients over pasta. Sprinkle with Parmesan, garnish with lemon and parsley.
If using dried pasta, cook ahead of time, drain and coat with oil to prevent stickiness.
If using fresh pasta, start cooking just before prawns and proscuitto are done.

Serves 4

See Glossary*

Grilled Marinated Chicken Breasts

4 whole boneless, skinless chicken breasts, cut into halves

Marinade (Yield: 2½ c.):
1 c. red wine vinegar
¼ c. grapefruit juice (preferably fresh squeezed)
1 T. garlic, minced
1 T. Dijon mustard
2 c. salad oil
1 T. dried rosemary
1 T. dried basil
salt and pepper to taste

Mustard sour cream sauce (Yield: 2 c.):
1½ c. sour cream
1 T. Dijon mustard
1 t. sugar
½ T. fresh garlic, minced
pinch salt
pinch white pepper
½ T parsley, chopped

Marinade: In a blender or food processor, combine vinegar, grapefruit juice, garlic and Dijon mustard. Start mixing slowly and add oil slowly, rosemary, basil and salt and pepper. (It should have a creamy look.) Place chicken breasts in tray, pour marinade over chicken and let marinate for 6 hours in refrigerator.
Mix mustard sour cream sauce ingredients well and chill until serving time. Remove chicken halves from marinade (don't wipe off excess). Grill until tender. Place on individual plates and cover with mustard sour cream sauce.

Serves 4

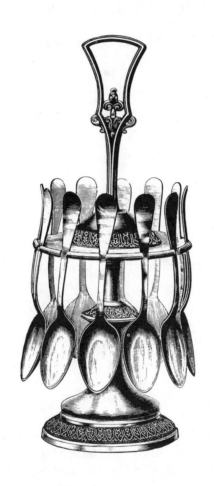

The Toll House

15301 Highway 253 • Boonville, California 95415
(707) 895-3630

Cradled in the pastoral beauty of the lovely Bell Valley and surrounded by rolling, sheep-dotted meadows, The Toll House Inn beckons invitingly. An old toll road passes by and lends its name to the historic Inn which was built in 1912 and renovated by Innkeeper, Beverly Nesbitt. Sunny hardwood floors, patios and comfortable verandas offer a welcome respite from hectic days. Relax in a tree-shaded hammock while gentle breezes rock you to sleep, or soak out the kinks in an outdoor spa sheltered by a gazebo. The tantalizing aroma of home-cured bacon and hot coffee wafts in the sweet morning air and the resident dog or cat pads quietly alongside as you follow your nose to breakfast. You've come home to the Toll House Inn.

Apple Dumplings

Pastry:

2 c. all-purpose flour
½ t. salt
½ c. Victor brand lard
¼ c. butter or margarine
1 T. white cider vinegar
½ c. ice water

Dumplings:

½ c. walnuts, finely chopped
2 T. raw sugar
¼ t. each cinnamon and nutmeg
3 T. butter, melted
6 small red Gravenstein apples, peeled and cored
1 egg, slightly beaten

Sauce:

1 jar butterscotch topping
1 c. orange juice
½ c. apple brandy

Pastry: In medium bowl combine flour and salt with pastry blender or hands. Cut in shortening and butter until mixture resembles coarse meal. Gradually add vinegar and water and stir with fork until moistened and pastry leaves side of bowl. Knead on flour-dusted board, divide dough into 6 balls, roll out on floured board into 6" squares.

Dumplings: In small bowl combine walnuts, sugar, cinnamon, nutmeg and melted butter. Spoon evenly into each apple cavity. Place each apple on each pastry square. Place between hands,

Apple Dumplings (con't)

molding pastry against apple. Seal seams with beaten egg wash. Place seam side down. Repeat with remaining apples and pastry. Save scraps of dough for decorative leaves if desired.

Preheat oven to 425 degrees. Brush entire pastry with egg wash. Place in 13" x 9" baking dish, being careful dumplings do not touch each other. Bake 15 minutes. Reduce heat to 375 degrees and bake 20 minutes more.

Sauce: In small saucepan, heat all sauce ingredients to boiling. Continue baking dumplings 15 minutes more, basting with the sauce occasionally. Serve warm with cream (whipped or plain).

Decorative leaves: Roll out pastry scraps. With sharp knife cut out small leaves. Make veins on leaves with blunt edge of knife. Roll a small piece of dough into a 2" long narrow rope. Cut into 6 ½" pieces for stems. Press leaves and stems to top center of each apple with dab of egg wash. Sprinkle with raw sugar granules.

Serves 6

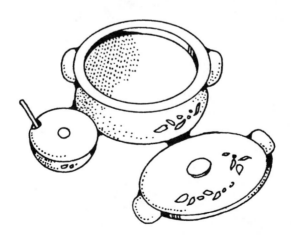

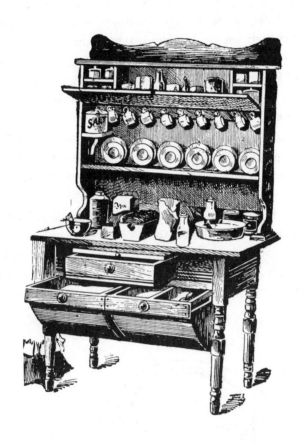

Philo Pottery Inn

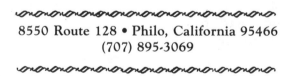

8550 Route 128 • Philo, California 95466
(707) 895-3069

Once used as a stage stop in the 19th century, the cool and airy Philo Pottery Inn offers more than just a weekend get-away. The Innkeepers have created a Bed and Breakfast Inn that brings together the rural beauty of the lush, green Anderson Valley and an innovative ceramic studio with accompanying log cabin gallery. Inside the Inn sunbeams filter through stained glass windows and illuminate four guest rooms with private decks, decorated with country collectables and handmade floor tiles from the ceramic studio. A Continental breakfast is served each morning. Before leaving don't forget to stop in the gallery and take home a memory from the Philo Pottery Inn.

Chicken Chaudfroid

4 whole boneless chicken breasts, halved
2 cans chicken broth
3 oz. cream cheese
4 T. mayonnaise
2 T lemon juice
½ t. lemon peel, grated
¼ t. salt
2 T. fresh dill, snipped

Cook chicken in broth 30 minutes or until tender; chill in broth in refrigerator until cool.
Make paste of remaining ingredients and coat rounded side of each chilled chicken breast half.

8 very thick slices peeled ripe tomato
romaine lettuce
seasoned salt
toasted, slivered almonds
fresh dill, snipped
ripe avocado, sliced in strips
clear French dressing

Assemble as follows: place tomato slice on romaine; sprinkle with salt; place chilled coated chicken on tomato slice and sprinkle with almonds and dill; garnish with avocado; drizzle French dressing over, as desired.

Serves 8

New England "Hash Browns"

1 lb. dry pea or navy beans
½ c. molasses
½ t. black pepper
1 t. dry mustard
¼ slab bacon, diced
⅓ c. onion, chopped

Rinse beans; in a large kettle combine beans and 2 quarts water. Bring to a boil; simmer 2 minutes. Remove from heat and let sit 1 hour. Bring to a boil again and simmer until beans are tender. Drain, reserving liquid. Mix molasses, black pepper, mustard and 2-3 c. reserved liquid.

In a 2 qt. bean pot, mix beans, diced bacon and onion. Stir in molasses mixture and bake at 300 degrees for 3½-4 hours, stirring occasionally, and adding more liquid if needed.

New England "Hash Browns" are a welcome and fun change from ordinary home fries or grits and go well with bacon and eggs for breakfast.

Serves 12

Mystery Bread

2 pkg. dry yeast
1 T. honey or molasses
⅓ c. warm water (105-115 degrees)
7 c. flour: mixture of white, whole wheat, 4 or 7 grain cereal
   (the cooking kind)
½ stick butter or margarine
2 t. salt (or less)
2 c. ice water

Stir yeast and honey or molasses into water in a 1 qt. measure; let stand 5-10 minutes. Use food processor dough blade to process flour, butter and salt for 20 seconds. Add ice water to the yeast mixture.

With processor running, pour liquid through feed tube in a steady stream as fast as flour mixture absorbs it (about 35 seconds). Continue processing until dough starts to clean inside of the workbowl, then run for 80 seconds more.

Shape dough into smooth ball, place in lightly floured plastic bag and squeeze out air, closing end with wire twist, allowing space for dough to rise. Let rise in warm place until doubled in size, about 1-½ hours.

Remove from bag, punch down. Shape into 3 loaves and place each in a 1 lb. loaf pan. Cover with oiled plastic wrap or a towel and let rise in a warm place until just above the top of the pans, about ¾ hour.

Bake on middle rack of a preheated 375 degree oven for 35 minutes or until brown on top. Remove from pans and cool on racks.

Yield: 3 1 lb. loaves

So called because it never comes out exactly the same...

354

Laura's Carrot Bran Muffins

1 c. bran flakes cereal, crushed
1 c. all purpose flour
¼ c. firmly packed light brown sugar
2 t. baking powder
½ t baking soda
½ t. cinnamon
¼ t. nutmeg
1 c. milk
1 egg
3 T. vegetable oil
1 c. carrots, grated
¼ c. walnuts, chopped
¼ c. raisins

Preheat oven to 400 degrees. Generously grease muffin tins. Combine first 7 ingredients in large bowl. Blend milk, egg and oil. Stir into dry ingredients, mixing well. Stir in carrots, walnuts, raisins. Spoon batter into prepared tins. Bake muffins until golden and toothpick inserted in center comes out clean, about 15-20 minutes. Remove from tins, cool slightly on racks and serve warm.

Variations: Mix 3 oz. of softened cream cheese, 2 t. of sugar and ¼ t. of vanilla in a small bowl. Before baking muffins, top each with a small dollop of the cream cheese mixture. Bake as directed above.

Yield: 12 muffins

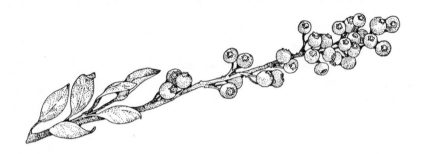

Dottie O'Neil's Temptation: Blueberry Muffins

3 ½ c. sifted all purpose flour
2 T. baking powder
¾ c. sugar
pinch salt (optional)
5 eggs, slightly beaten
½ c. milk
5 oz. unsalted butter or margarine, melted and cooled
4-5 c. blueberries, fresh or frozen
   (wild blueberries are best and can be bought frozen)
additional sugar for topping

Preheat oven to 425 degrees. Mix dry ingredients together; stir in eggs, milk, butter; do not overmix. Carefully stir in berries. Grease the top of large muffin tins. Insert paper cups and spoon batter to the top of the paper cups. Sprinkle generously with sugar. Reduce heat to 400 degrees, place muffin tins on middle shelf of oven. Bake about 25 minutes, until muffins are golden brown. Remove from tins and cool.

Yield: 15 to 18 muffins

Familiar Chocolate Chip Cookies "Mrs. Fields"

2 c. butter
2 c. sugar
2 c. brown sugar
4 eggs
2 t. vanilla
4 c. flour
5 c. ground oatmeal (measure after grinding)
1 t. salt
2 t. baking powder
2 t. baking soda
24 oz. chocolate chips
1 8 oz. Hershey bar, grated
3 c. nuts, chopped

Cream butter and sugars; add eggs and vanilla, then flour. Add oatmeal, salt, baking powder, baking soda and mix well. Add chocolate chips, Hershey and nuts.
Bake at 375 degrees for 6 minuttes (may take a little longer).

Yield: 112 cookies

Glossary

BROWN SAUCE (quick) - Bring 2 c. beef stock to a boil and then simmer for 15 minutes. Add 2 T. cornstarch or arrowroot dissolved in 3 T. cold water and cook over moderate heat, stirring constantly, until thickened. Then simmer for 5 minutes.

CHOUX PASTE (CREAM PUFF PASTE) - Bring 1 c. water and 6 T. butter (cut into pieces), 1 t. salt and a pinch of nutmeg. Boil slowly until the butter has melted. Remove from heat and pour in 1 c. sifted flour, mix thoroughly. Then beat over medium high heat 1 to 2 minutes and make a well in the center. Break 4 eggs in center and beat until the eggs are absorbed. Fill pastry bag with dough and squeeze the paste onto a baking sheet. Bake in a preheated 425 degree oven for 20 minutes. Cool the puffs on a rack.

CLARIFIED BUTTER - Heat whole butter very slowly. Remove white deposit that forms on top. Strain the butter through a sieve into a small bowl, leaving the milky solids in the bottom of the pan. Store uncovered in refrigerator, as it will keep indefinitely.

CREAM ANGLAISE - Beat 6 egg yolks and add ⅓ c. sugar, 1 T. at a time. Add a pinch of salt. Whisk until mixture ribbons when the whisk is lifted. Add 2 c. scalded milk and keep whisking. Transfer to saucepan and cook over moderate heat, whisking until thick. Remove from heat and stir in 2 t. vanilla. Strain custard in small bowl. Set in larger bowl filled with cracked ice and let cool. Stir; chill the sauce, covered.

CREAM FRAICHE - (heavy cream that has been allowed to ferment slightly). To make your own, combine 2 parts heavy cream to 1 part sour cream or buttermilk. Cover bowl and set out at room temperature about 4 hours. Then refrigerate until ready to use.

DEGLAZE - Pour wine into pan in which food has been prepared in butter (food has been removed and just the pan juices remain).

DEMI GLAZE (quick brown sauce) - Bring 2 c. beef stock to boil and them simmer for 15 minutes. Add 2 T. arrowroot dissolved in 3 T. cold water and heat, stirring constantly, until thickened for 5 minutes.

Glossary (con't)

FUMET - A fish stock used as a base for sauces.

LIME OR LEMON ZEST - The grated outer covering of lemon or lime, just the skin part, as the white part becomes bitter.

PANCETTA - Dry-cured unsmoked bacon, available in gourmet and specialty food stores.

PESTO - In a food processor, combine ½ c. fresh basil and ½ c. fresh parsley. Add 2 cloves of garlic, ¼ c. Parmesan cheese, ¼ c. olive oil and ¼ c. pine nuts, season with salt and pepper. Blend.

ROUX (mixture of butter and flour) - Melt butter in sauce pan, add flour slowly and whisk until thick.

Wine Glossary

ACID - A naturally occurring and essential component of wine that provides freshness, balance and potential for longevity. A good balance between acid and sugar is sought in the grapes at harvest and in the finished wine.

AGING - The process of bringing wine to a point where it is judged ready for market. If storage conditions are right and the wine has the components for longevity, aging can go on for years in the bottle. Red varietal wines usually age well, and some white varietals also can have long lives.

APPELLATION OF ORIGIN - The geographical origin of wine, always stated clearly and prominently on the wine label. These geographical regions, or appellations, are designated by the Federal Government based upon several criteria, among them that the area produces grapes and wines that are unique to it in some demonstrable way. The appellation may cover an area as large as the United States and as small or smaller than the Napa Valley.

AROMA - The olfactory sensation (smell) of a wine that is directly related to the grape from which it is made (see BOUQUET and NOSE).

BARREL FERMENTATION - Meaning that a wine was fermented totally or partially in a small oak barrel.

BERRY - The individual grape within a cluster, or bunch, of grapes. A term used interchangeably with grape in the wine and winegrape industry.

BLEND - As a noun, blend may refer to any mixture of wines from different varietals, different vintages or different appellations of origin. Within a winery, blend may also refer to a "master blend," wherein specific proportions of different lots of the same wine are used to achieve a particular style or personality of wine.

BLOOM - The stage in each growing season, usually late spring or early summer, when grapevines blossom with small flowers and self-pollination occurs.

BOTRYTIS CINEREA - A mold that affects grapes when weather conditions are within certain ranges of warmth and humidity. When it occurs late in the growing season under these specific conditions, the mold causes the grape skins to shrivel and brown and the natural grape sugars to concentrate. Under these beneficial conditions, botrytis is called the 'noble rot'. It results in wonderfully luscious and sweet dessert wines that cannot be achieved under any other conditions, either artificial or natural.

Wine Glossary (con't)

BOUQUET - The olfactory sensation of a wine that is a direct result of its cooperage and aging.

BRIX - A term used to express a standard measurement of soluble solids (sugar) content in grapes. Expressed as degrees of Brix, it is an indication of ripeness in the grapes and the potential alcohol content of the finished wine.

BUD - As a noun, a small node or lump on the mature cane of a grapevine from which shoots grow in the spring. As a verb, refers to the act of budding or grafting wood from one vine onto another.

BUD BREAK - An event that signals the beginning of the annual growing season of a grapevine. Usually occurring in late winter or early spring, new buds break through the woody surface of the vine, indicating both the time when the vines will flower and the time when the grapes will reach maturity for harvest.

CANE - A mature shoot of one-year-old wood on a grapevine.

CAP - A crusty layer of grape skins, pulp and seeds that forms on top of a red varietal wine during fermentation.

CELLAR - As a noun, that area within a winery where wines are made and aged. As a verb, refers to cellaring or aging bottled wine.

CELLARMASTER - The person who is chief of production in a winery, in charge of operations and looking to the winemaster for direction.

CHARACTER - A term for distinguishing features that are collectively an integrated expression of what makes one wine different from another.

COMPLEXITY - A term that connotes a number of discernible characteristics in a wine. The overall sensation of a wine, derived from all of its features, its components, its characteristics. Fruit, winemaking style and cooperage are examples of factors that contribute to a wine's complexity.

COOPERAGE - Containers of any size or material that hold wine before it is bottled.

CRUSH - The activity that occurs immediately after grapes are harvested—they are taken to the winery to be crushed. The terms 'harvest' and 'crush' are frequently used interchangeably to describe the culmination of a growing season, when the grapes are harvested, transported to the winery and made into wine.

Wine Glossary (con't)

CUVEE - A French term applicable primarily to Champagne and sparkling wines. It refers to the specific blend of still wines used in the second fermentation process.

DRY WINE - A wine without perceptible sweetness, generally below .5% residual sugar.

ENOLOGY - The science of winemaking. Also oenology.

FERMENTATION - The process by which yeast converts grape juice to alcohol.

FILTRATION - The process of passing wine through a porous material at various stages of development to remove suspended natural solid materials.

FINING - A process in which clays or protein, such as raw egg whites, are passed through the wine as clarifying agents. The fining material settles to the bottom, and is removed with the sediments.

FREE RUN - The fresh grape juice which is collected and available for fermentation prior to pressing the grapes for further juice extraction.

FROST PROTECTION - Various methods for preventing frost from damaging grapevines, by using vineyard heaters, overhead sprinklers or wind machines, individually or in combination.

GENERIC - Describes wines not bearing names of the grapes from which they were made. In the U.S., examples of such wines are Chablis, Burgundy or Rosé.

GONDOLA - A large, wheeled, open trailer in which grapes are transported from vineyards to wineries for crushing.

LATE HARVEST - A term used for grapes that are allowed to stay on vines well past the primary harvest season, with or without Botrytis Cinerea mold. Grape sugars concentrate in the berries through dehydration, resulting in a luscious sweet wine. Late harvest wines vary in sweetness depending upon the sugar content of the grapes at time of harvest. Labeling laws are exacting regarding the use of the terms Late Harvest, Select Late Harvest and Special Select Late Harvest, each of which denotes a minimum harvest sugar level.

LIMOUSIN - The name of a government-owned forest in France that is a source of oak used to make cooperage of various sizes for aging wine.

Wine Glossary (con't)

METHODE CHAMPENOISE - The classic method of producing high-quality champagne and sparkling wines in which a second fermentation takes place in the same bottle in which the wine is sold.

MICROCLIMATE - An area, generally small, defined by topography, climate, soil type and other environmental elements. A microclimate possesses singular features unto itself which will affect the qualities and character of a wine produced from grapes grown within its borders.

MUST - The combination of juice, pulp, seeds and skins of grapes as they leave the crusher and go into the fermentation tank.

NEVERS - Another government-owned forest in France that provides oak for wine aging cooperage.

NOSE - The overall olfactory sensation of a particular wine, good or bad, encompassing both its aroma (from the grape) and its bouquet (from cooperage and aging).

pH - A measurable factor in wine and in grapes that indicates the activity of acid. pH is a factor that controls elements in wine that may lead to longevity and is ultimately the most important factor in choosing the time to harvest grapes.

PHYLLOXERA VASTATRIX - A root louse that attacks the roots of grapevines and eventually kills them. In the Napa Valley, and in most of the European wine regions, most vines grow on phylloxera-resistant rootstock.

POMACE - The dry residue of skins, seeds and pulp from pressed wine.

PRESS - Equipment used to recover either the fresh grape juice after crushing, or wine out of the fermented must, or both.

PRUNING - Trimming the dormant grapevines during winter; also called 'removing the brush'. Pruning is the primary method used for managing the crop level, by leaving a pre-determined number of buds on each cane.

PUMPING OVER - The act of pumping red wine from the bottom of a fermentation tank into the top of the tank, over the cap, to develop even color extraction and aerate the wine as it ferments, thus aiding fermentation.

RACKING - The process of moving wine from one cooperage to another.

Wine Glossary (con't)

REFRACTOMETER - A device that measures the soluble solids (sugar) content of grapes and other fruit, and reads it out in degrees of Brix.

RESIDUAL SUGAR - The unfermented grape sugars remaining in a finished wine, indicating its degree of sweetness. Residual sugar is frequently indicated on the wine label by weight or degrees Brix.

ROOTSTOCK - The roots and woody stem of non-fruiting grape varieties onto which specific winegrape varieties are grafted. Such rootstock is generally chosen for its resistance to soil pests such as phylloxera or nematodes, but is also selected for its particular growth characteristics, its adaption to particular soils and its affinity for the type of grape to be grown.

SKIN CONTACT - Refers to the crushed skins of grapes remaining with the fresh grape juice before pressing. The amount of time allowed for skin contact is a decision that affects some aspects of finished wine, such as color or tannins.

SPARKLING WINES - Wines that undergo a second fermentation, usually in the bottle, resulting in effervescence.

SWEET WINES - Wines that contain perceptible percentages of residual sugar. The threshold for perceiving sweetness is about .5 to .7% residual sugar. Wine with 1% or more residual sugar will taste sweet. Some of the classic finished dessert wines may have as much as 32% residual sugar.

TANNIN - A group of organic substances in grape skins, seeds and stems. Tannin is responsible for the astringent, puckery quality in some young wines. Tannin is present in virtually all wines but is generally more pronounced in red wines.

TRONCAIS - Another government-owned forest in France which produces oak for wine cooperage.

VARIETAL - A wine produced totally or primarily from one specific grape variety and which bears the name of that variety; Cabernet Sauvignon, Chardonnay, Sauvignon Blanc, Zinfandel, etc. In order to bear that name on its label, the wine must contain a minimum of 75% of the varietal named.

VARIETY - The botanical name for a specific type of grapevine, such as Chardonnay, for example.

Wine Glossary (con't)

VERAISON - The beginning of ripening. An occurrence in unripe grapes when they turn from green to purple, or in the case of white varieties, from green to translucent green, yellow or gold. This is also the time when sugar content begins to increase. Veraison is a point in time from which the time of harvest can be predicted with some accuracy.

VINIFICATION - The process of producing wine from grapes; winemaking.

VINTAGE - A word with several meanings. The most widely understood meaning applies to the picking of grapes at harvest and making wine with those grapes. Thus, a vintage wine is one that is produced in a particular year.

VINTNER - In the U.S., vintner has come to mean the principal of a winery, especially if that person is involved to one degree or another in the winemaking process.

VITICULTURE - The science and practice of growing grapes.

Courtesy of Napa Valley Vintners Association

Index

A

B

C

D

E

F

G

N

O

375

Q - R

378

T

FRONT COVER:	Steve Doty
LITERARY COMMENTS:	Jane Clydesdale
TYPESETTING:	Paul Tapia Studios
PHOTOGRAPHER:	Don Saxton
PRINTING:	Publisher Press, Inc.
PROOFREADING:	Anne Witzleben

For comments, re-orders, the address of your nearest distributor, or information on starting a restaurant guide for your city, please contact:

The Tastes of Tahoe
P.O. Box 6114
Incline Village, NV 89450
(702) 831-5182

THE TASTES Of TAHOE

The Tastes of Tahoe
P.O. Box 6114
Incline Village, NV 89450

Please send _____ copies of **The Tastes of Tahoe II** at .... $7.95 each.

Please send _____ copies of **The Tastes of Marin** at .... $7.95 each.

Please send _____ copies of **The Tastes of California Wine Country - Napa/Sonoma** at .... $9.95 each.

Please send _____ copies of **Cooking INN Style** at .... $9.95 each.

Please send _____ copies of **The Tastes of California Wine Country - North Coast** at .... $11.95 each.

Please send _____ copies of **The Best of the Tastes of Tahoe** at .... $11.95 each.

Add $1.50 postage and handling for the first book ordered and .50¢ for each additional book.

Enclosed is my check for _____

Name _____

Address _____

City _____ State _____ Zip _____

☐ This is a gift. Send directly to:

Name _____

Address _____

City _____ State _____ Zip _____

☐ Autographed by the author.

Autographed to: _____

The Tastes of Tahoe
P.O. Box 6114
Incline Village, NV 89450

Please send _____ copies of **The Tastes of Tahoe II** at .... $7.95 each.

Please send _____ copies of **The Tastes of Marin** at .... $7.95 each.

Please send _____ copies of **The Tastes of California Wine Country - Napa/Sonoma** at .... $9.95 each.

Please send _____ copies of **Cooking INN Style** at .... $9.95 each.

Please send _____ copies of **The Tastes of California Wine Country - North Coast** at .... $11.95 each.

Please send _____ copies of **The Best of the Tastes of Tahoe** at .... $11.95 each.

Add $1.50 postage and handling for the first book ordered and .50¢ for each additional book.

Enclosed is my check for _____

Name _____

Address _____

City _____ State _____ Zip _____

☐ This is a gift. Send directly to:

Name _____

Address _____

City _____ State _____ Zip _____

☐ Autographed by the author.

Autographed to: _____

THE TASTES OF TAHOE

The Tastes of Tahoe
P.O. Box 6114
Incline Village, NV 89450

Please send _____ copies of **The Tastes of Tahoe II** at .... $7.95 each.

Please send _____ copies of **The Tastes of Marin** at .... $7.95 each.

Please send _____ copies of **The Tastes of California Wine Country - Napa/Sonoma** at .... $9.95 each.

Please send _____ copies of **Cooking INN Style** at .... $9.95 each.

Please send _____ copies of **The Tastes of California Wine Country - North Coast** at .... $11.95 each.

Please send _____ copies of **The Best of the Tastes of Tahoe** at .... $11.95 each.

Add $1.50 postage and handling for the first book ordered and .50¢ for each additional book.

Enclosed is my check for _____

Name _____

Address _____

City _____ State _____ Zip _____

☐ This is a gift. Send directly to:

Name _____

Address _____

City _____ State _____ Zip _____

☐ Autographed by the author.

Autographed to: _____

ABOUT THE AUTHOR

Sonnie Imes, a native of Philadelphia, Pennsylvania, has lived in Incline Village, Nevada on the North Shore of Lake Tahoe for the past 11 years. A restaurant voyeur and regarded by some as the "Dr. Ruth of Cuisine" presents this, her eighth book.

Sonnie produced and directed her own television show on PBS, "A Taste of Tahoe," featuring chefs from area restaurants who prepared gourmet specialties on the air and has taught various cooking classes for Sierra Nevada College. While researching her next book "The Tastes of Cruising," she has lectured and given food demonstrations on cruise ships.

Sonnie's long range plan is a desire to travel the country and create restaurant guides for various areas, specializing in the elements which make each unique.

Notes

Notes

Notes

Notes

Notes